HAUNTED SPRINGFIELD MISSOURI

EDWARD & KAREN UNDERWOOD, WITH JOHN & SHERRY JONES

Haunted America

Published by Haunted America
A Division of The History Press
Charleston, SC 29403
www.historypress.net

Photographs by Heather Stanley
Illustrations by John Jones

First published 2014

Manufactured in the United States

ISBN 978.1.62619.120.4

Library of Congress CIP data applied for.

Notice: The information in this book is true and complete to the best of our knowledge. It is offered without guarantee on the part of the author or The History Press. The author and The History Press disclaim all liability in connection with the use of this book.

Dead-ication

This book is dedicated to the lost souls of the Queen City and the unholy aftermath of the Council of Elders.

CONTENTS

Contents

FOREWORD

Greetings, my friends! As a longtime native of Springfield, I have many a local tale and urban legend tucked away just for those special dark and mildly humid nights. For instance, there's the time when MoMo (Missouri's own Bigfoot) trashed my RV in a drunken stupor and refused to pay for the damages. Or the summer of 1953, when a crate of venomous cobras slithered their way into people's yards but by winter quickly and anticlimactically died without biting anyone.

But none of these tales will be found here, for it just so happens that this book is about ghost stories, which are right up my alley! I'm a TV horror host (broadcasting from the terrifying heart of the Missouri Ozarks)—so I've got some experience in the field of what scares people. In my humble opinion, the scariest stories on the market are the ghost stories. Oh, your vampires are all right, your werewolves are mildly deserving of attention and your Frankensteins are somewhat arresting. But ghost stories? Turn down the lights, close the curtains and put that flashlight under your chin, and suddenly the world of the supernatural seems very close and very eerily possible. Nobody ever scares their campfire comrades by telling mummy stories.

Every area has its own distinctive ghost stories, and the authors of this book have put together some of the most extraordinary ghost stories that float around the area in this fun little collection. If you're ready for a cold tingle to run down your spine—read on! Until next time,

Bad Day, Bad Night, Bad Dreams!

—"Uncle Gregory"

Check out "The New Uncle Gregory Horror Hour" on KOZL-27 in Springfield, Missouri, or visit facebook.com/UncleGregoryHorror.

Welcome to Haunted Springfield. Bundle up, it's going to be a chilling journey.

PREFACE

This is our third book on the topic of obscure history, the second specifically devoted to the strange goings-on in places believed to be haunted. We have started two history-ghost tours in two states and personally walked hundreds of people to the locations of some of the more famous local sites where bizarre events took place and, in some cases, reportedly still take place!

Once again, we have met with some very interesting people who have graciously told us their personal ghost stories. Most of these stories flow easily and relate a supernatural event that happened to a friend, relative or someone they used to know. However, a few of them are personal, firsthand experiences that seem to have taken a toll on the storytellers.

We are always grateful to those brave souls who risk ridicule and rejection (which never come from us!) to tell us about experiences that go beyond the normal course of mortal life. We are especially grateful to two individuals, who wish to remain unnamed, for two of the most bizarre ghost stories we have ever heard and access to the physical artifacts that are directly connected to these amazing tales.

During our research for this book, we discovered a twisted little tale that filled in a gap in local history and seems consistent with some unusual turns in the city's government. Perhaps we have found a missing element to understanding part of the development of Springfield, Missouri.

We are also grateful to our co-workers and coauthors John and Sherry Jones. These two are clever people, quick thinkers and a joy to collaborate with. John's illustrations give this book a classic spooky feel and allow us to fill in some blanks for things that could never be photographed. John and Sherry plan to continue collecting ghost stories and are currently trying to buy a haunted house.

It is our sincere hope that in these pages you will find some delightfully spine-tingling adventures, as well as some mostly forgotten history about a marvelous American city called Springfield.

—EDWARD AND KAREN UNDERWOOD

This is the first book we have ever written. It is not overstating things to say that not one word of this book would have happened without our friends, co-workers and likeminded lovers of the shadowy side of life, Edward and Karen Underwood.

Sherry and I have always had a fascination with things haunted. One of our goals in life is to own a genuinely haunted house. While living in Springfield, Missouri, we saw many truly scary things and participated in many horrifying events. Some of the things we saw can never be explained, and many things we experienced should never be shared. We hope this collection of stories will give you an appreciation for our area's fascinating history and impart to you the gift of countless nightmares.

—JOHN AND SHERRY JONES

ACKNOWLEDGEMENTS

First, we want to thank all the folks who took the time to share their Springfield ghost stories with us. Ghost stories pass from person to person, and unless they are captured and written down, they most likely vanish like the phantom spirits they often describe.

A huge thank-you has to go out to the Springfield librarians and schoolteachers who helped us track down more than just a few elusive facts and dates. We couldn't do this kind of work without the cooperation of those who know where such obscure information can be found.

We also owe a nod to the Internet and its immediate access to the stories of so many people from so many different perspectives and time periods. And finally, a great big scary hug to TV's Uncle Gregory for his foreword. We salute his continuing efforts to entertain and terrify the entire city of Springfield, Missouri.

A Word About Ghosts

Before we pull back the curtain on this collection of ghost stories that shed a strangely colored light on the darker side of the city of Springfield, Missouri, we want to take an opportunity to discuss some these famous disembodies souls that walk through history.

In our reading audience, we undoubtedly have both advocates of all things paranormal and skeptics who stand ever ready to dispute and deny the existence of anything that cannot be seen, touched and tested.

It is not the intent or purpose of this book to make anyone adopt any belief system. The tales we share are done in the interest of entertainment and history. Please do not be offended by anything you read here. Conversely, do not attempt to start a new religious sect based on anything you read here.

We always like to point out to our ghost tour audiences that ghosts are universal. From an anthropological perspective, they are historical gold. When we know your ghost stories, we know your values, your fears and how you relate the past to the future. There is no culture on the face of the earth that does not have ghost stories, and there has been no time in history when they did not flourish.

We started the Springfield Mystery Tour with a Bible verse: "But when the disciples saw him walking on the sea, they were terrified, and said, 'It is a ghost!' and they cried out in fear." That is Matthew 14:26, and the purpose of our Bible lesson is to show you how every culture has knowledge of the concept of ghosts. In this verse, we see the men who were raised in orthodox Jewish homes calling on their backgrounds to fill in the gaps in what they were witnessing. There was no logical explanation, so they inserted that mysterious *something* they had been told about since they were young. They inserted the concept of a ghost.

Even these properly schooled godly folk had a ready ghost concept handy for just such an occasion. Every culture in every era has had a fascination with life after death and the question of the soul's consciousness and ability outside the body. That's basically where ghosts come from. In our inner beliefs, we feel there must be more to the value and meaning of existence than the mere years on earth. This quest to know and to prove that the universe is just and that good is not forgotten and evil does not go unpunished also plays into our ghost concepts.

In the late 1800s, when the religion of spiritualism was growing rapidly and giving traditional Christianity a run for its money in terms of sheer popularity, people sought evidence of spirits. They used an upside-down wine glass and slips of paper with letters, numbers and words on them placed around the table. Then everyone would put their fingertips on the base of the inverted glass and ask questions of the departed. Shockingly the glass would move to the letters and spell out words to spell those answers. That's right—it was a Ouija board long before Parker Brothers made plastic planchettes.

Today, we have replaced such silly things with scientific instruments. Electromagnetic field detectors, digital motion sensors, heat image cameras and some truly strange devices like random word generators are the modern version of rapping noises, wine glass divination and pendulum swings. The one startling thing all of these methods share is that the information provided by them is completely subjective in interpretation. In other words, one man's message from the great beyond is another man's loose electrical wire or creaky window shutter.

We can all agree that ghost stories stir our imaginations. They create a sense of wonder over the past and give us hope for the future. So regardless of your personal paranormal penchants, let's open that old squeaky door, brush away the cobwebs and step into the dark and shadowy world of ghosts and unexplained visions.

Springfield, Missouri, is known as the queen city of the Ozarks and the birthplace of Route 66. The land now known as Missouri was a chunk of the Louisiana Purchase in 1803. It became a state on August 10, 1821. The city of Springfield was founded in 1830 and incorporated in 1838.

As to how the town got its name, there seems to be a choice of folklore options available to you. One version of the story holds that the town was

Downtown Springfield is a hotbed of activity and culture.

named for a spring that ran under the hill upon which the major part of the town resided, in a field. Hence Springfield!

Another version says that when the town's appointed bigwigs gathered to discuss incorporating the town, a man known as Kindred Rose proposed Springfield in honor of his old hometown in Tennessee. That is a good, logical and even sentimental story about how a town got its name.

But I know another one, an even better one. An alternate version of the story holds that a man named James Wilson simply offered everyone large quantities of whiskey to vote the name of the town Springfield in honor of his old hometown of Springfield, Massachusetts.

Well, the last story is much more colorful, and for our cause, it has the added benefit that his barrel of booze brings us to the subject of "spirits." Sure, it's a bit of a stretch, but for a city as haunted as Springfield, nothing should be out of the question.

In the following chapters, we will unfold for you the tales of terror and strange, otherworldly phenomena that have become part of the history and culture of this remarkable city. Prepare to be amazed, challenged and perhaps just shocked by some of Springfield's most notorious ghost stories.

CHAPTER 1

GHOSTS ACT UP IN THEATERS

In our many travels to see places that have been identified as haunted, there is one consistent type of location that will have ghost stories in virtually every city, in every state: theaters.

I have come to the conclusion that this is true for three reasons. Number one: theaters are usually old buildings with lots of rooms, beams, braces and walls that have heavy scenery, lights or other objects hanging on or from them. This can account for a lot of strange creaking, cracking and various howling wind sounds. Number two: those who work in these places are given to the dramatic. They love story, plot and premise and have wonderful imaginations. This is why they work in theater, and this is how they are able to draw an audience into a performance. Number three: theaters are places where tremendous emotional energy is expelled. Think about it—the actors all feel the plights of the characters they play and spend that emotional energy, and the audience follows suit. They laugh, they cry, they think and they feel along with the show. Special occasions are spent in theaters. How many have been taken to the theater to celebrate a birthday or an anniversary? And think of how many couples have taken advantage of that upper balcony area to get to know each other a little better.

My point is that if we can trace the incidents of ghosts being linked to a past event that leaves a residual energy impression on the place where that energy was expended, then theaters are a wonderland of spent energy. So it is no surprise that our nation's theaters have as many ghost stories attached to them as graveyards and battlefields do. And one of the most haunted theaters in America has to be the Landers Theatre in Springfield.

John and Douglas Landers led the effort to design and build the ultimate theater facility for Springfield. They designed it in Napoleon's Renaissance architectural style and opened it in 1909. The Landers Theatre gave Springfield residents the finest vaudeville performers in the country, including Lon Chaney and Fanny Brice.

In 1920, a fire killed a janitor and nearly destroyed the entire structure. A man named Ensley Barbour took up the cause of rebuilding the theater, and it opened again in 1922. By that time, vaudeville starts were sharing the stage with silent movies, and in 1927, the Landers was one of the first theaters to join the technological revolution that was "talkies" when it pulled back the curtain and played Al Jolson in *The Jazz Singer* for a disbelieving audience.

The top floors of the theater were rented as studio space for radio station WIBM through the 1960s. But as America's downtown centers began to

The Landers Theatre is the home of Springfield Little Theatre Company. And according to local folklore, it is a very haunted place.

fade, the theater fell on hard times and was bought out by the Springfield Little Theatre Company in 1970.

This dynamic and committed community group raised money through multiple creative fund drives to take the building through several restoration stages. The group ultimately returned the Landers to its 1909 glory. Today, the theater company produces a remarkable series of plays each season. The Landers is also home to four of the most famous and well-documented ghosts in all of the Ozarks.

The janitor who died in the 1920 fire seems to have returned to work when the theater reopened in 1922. He is usually seen sweeping and working up in the balconies by the actors on the stage. He has been witnessed by people of every age group and cultural background, and the description of him is always shockingly consistent. It's also worth pointing out that the balcony is always very, very clean as well.

The second ghost is really a "two-for-one" situation. Apparently, in the earliest days of the theater, a young mother dropped her baby over the balcony railing to its death on the seats below. Some have seen a shimmering vision of this woman and the falling child loop over and over again inside the auditorium—sometimes even during a show. Others say that they hear only the sound of the mother gasping and the baby hitting the ground level and crying, followed by the comforting sounds of the mother. This phenomenon will repeat over and over several times in a row until it just stops. Our research could find no law enforcement record of the incident, but we did get one official to confirm that there was an infant fatality in the building. However, no further details could be obtained.

The third ghost is one that has only been seen by people standing on the street outside the front of the theater. Since the theater reopened in 1922, people on the street have often reported seeing a person with long blonde hair dressed in Elizabethan costume gazing down at them from the fourth-floor windows. Several attempts have apparently been made to find the person in the window from the inside, but no person is visible to anyone on the inside the building. One ghost hunter suggested that it could be a residual energy manifesting as a trapped reflection. Perhaps it is there all the time but only visible to observers when certain light refraction happens at the angle down on the street.

The fourth ghost is an unidentified man who appears standing in the middle of the auditorium. He looks around the room and vanishes again. Some believe this man occasionally manifests as a four or five foot tall green orb of light or haze that floats about the building. Others say he sometimes

The fourth-floor window is where one of the most common ghost sightings in Springfield occurs.

appears as a "black void," an area of the room that is like a black hole. It moves around the room and across the ceiling as a completely black space with nothing showing around or behind it.

Now, if these folks are right, the Landers has four ghosts—five, if you count the baby separate from the mother. However, if they are wrong about the last one, then the Landers Theatre has at least seven ghosts. You do the math.

CHAPTER 2

CORNER OF HEAVEN AND HELL

In the city of Springfield, there are many schools, educational institutions and colleges. The largest and most famous of colleges is Missouri State University, with over twenty thousand students and a favorable ranking in Princeton Review's "Best Colleges by Region" listing for several years in a row.

There are also no less than a dozen institutions devoted to education with a religious and theological emphasis. These dispensaries of deity-based worldviews include the Assemblies of God (AOG) Theological Seminary. Springfield is the headquarters for the denomination, which has produced such luminary cultural figures as Jim and Tammy Faye Baker, Jimmy Swaggart and Richard Dortch. You may remember these names from the 1980s televangelist sex scandals.

If you have a better memory, you might recall Aimee Semple McPherson, the fiery female evangelist whose mysterious five-week kidnapping or disappearance or wild romp with a lover still puzzles those who seek out her bizarre personal history. The AOG also gave us Paul and Jan Crouch and the TBN television network, with its spray-painted gold throne chairs for show hosts, and Benny Hinn, the big arena preacher who has apparently received from heaven the invaluable spiritual gift of making people fall down when he waves his hand or his suit coat at them.

Also under the affiliation of this prestigious denomination is Evangel University. This eighty-acre campus was part of the property of the former O'Reilly General Hospital. This army hospital treated over 100,000 patients through the World War II era. After the war, it was a veterans' hospital for a

The historic downtown square is home to many popular dining and entertainment attractions, including the Gilloiz Theatre, the Moxie Cinema and the Landers Theatre. In the middle of all this activity is the old downtown square.

short time until the military decided to divest itself of the property. In 1954, the Assemblies of God felt the leading of the Lord to buy the abandoned hospital. The last army hospital building was replaced in 2009.

The intention was to create a college that would heal the spiritually sick and further the AOG's vision of raising up a mighty, mighty army of powerful spiritual warriors to battle the evil onslaught of secular knowledge and information coming from the mere mortal colleges in the region.

But being in the Bible belt part of our nation's wardrobe, Springfield's idea of higher learning also means learning all the way up to heaven and possibly beyond. The Assembly of God denomination prides itself on both moral absolutes and spiritual elasticity.

For example, a moral absolute laid out in the AOG belief statement is that the Bible is the authoritative revelation from God and is true in every word. But the group also leaves room for personal spiritual revelation and interpretation. This point of spiritual schizophrenia might be part of the reason for our next ghost story.

In these halls of heavenly higher learning once prowled a professor. This man was a professor at the college because he failed as a pastor and as a traveling evangelist. These failures hit him so hard personally that he slowly became the complete opposite of everything he set out to be in the beginning. Instead of loving and full of joy, he unraveled into a very bitter, angry and petty person.

This caused him to lose not only the church he served but also his relationships with other ministers, evangelists and his own immediate family. His wife left him, though she never divorced him. The divorce would have been a further blow to whatever ministry career he had left to pursue.

The result of his hardened soul was that he dealt very severely with the students at the university. He was known as a "hardcore" teacher, an angry perfectionist with a sadistic bent. The main manifestation of his cruelty was the little brown leather notebook he carried. The very sight of this unassuming personal accessory caused stress in the students. It was in this well-worn tome that this professor kept his notes about and to students and even other faculty.

He would make these notes constantly—during classes, while walking down the hallways and even in the restrooms. Some notes were apparently scrawled for his own remembrance, but others—the majority of them—were meant for whoever had become the current target of his mean-spirited ritual.

The professor would stop whatever he was doing and scowl. Next, that ever-present little brown leather notebook would come into view, along with a red marking pen. Letters, words and sentences would be formed by obviously angry pen strokes, and a look of utter disdain would deepen over his unpleasant face before the note was ripped from the book and delivered to its target.

These little bits of venom would always be delivered at the worst possible time—or so it seemed to the students. If a young man had struck up a pleasant conversation with a young lady, the professor would intrude with his steely cold reprimands. If another instructor allowed a paper to be turned in late or eased the grading curve on an exam, surely the spoiler would come in front of the entire faculty in the lounge.

Even board members and executive administrators were not immune to his actions. In time, of course, he became a much-hated man by both his students and his co-workers. How could they express Christian love to this most unlikeable, unlovable man? Herein lays the heart of the aforementioned spiritual schizophrenia. In a normal world, someone would punch this arrogant clown in the nose. But in this domain, he was tolerated as one who allegedly had some sort of calling or authority to dole out these comments.

Why? Well, the answer lies in the content of the notes. They were angry, intolerant, critical rants aimed at every little aspect of someone's behavior, attitude or actions—but they were Bible based. For instance, a common note the professor gave out to students said, "Do not forsake the admonition or correction of the Lord," and another read "Turn ye away from foolish things." The insults were in the archaic language sent out with a distinctly "holier than thou" attitude. Consequently, what might have been immediately rejected outside the Christian bubble world was tolerated and even embraced as perhaps coming from God.

The professor knew this about the world he was scowling his way through and took full advantage of it. Perhaps he was a prophet. Perhaps he was the voice of one crying in the wilderness, not making friends but speaking deep wisdom in a world of silly-minded sinners. Perhaps the fact that you hated seeing him and that his notes shamed you was, in fact, proof that he was right and that you deserved to be reprimanded. Such logic allowed him to serve up his rancor to anyone.

At some point, his notes turned even more judgmental. Instead of these simple embarrassing admonitions, they began to play the hell card. Yes, his notes now breeched the topic of whether the recipient was worthy of heaven. This caused some to question as to whether he was losing his mind. However, that thought was always tempered by the next thought that he may say these things because he was genuinely prompted by God. And if that was the case, who would want to contradict him or defend the person in question? No one would.

At this point, the professor took up the habit of remaining in his office long after school hours, toiling away on his work. Just what this work consisted of was anyone's guess. Occasionally, the janitor would look in on him and see him bent over his desk with red pen in hand, feverishly writing in his notebook and ripping the pages out one after another after another. There were angry red ripped notes all over the top of his desk and all across the floor of his spacious office. The janitor reported this to the dean of the department, but no one was aware of any action that was taken to address the man's behavior.

Many students and co-workers found themselves being handed jagged scraps of paper with red letters saying "turn or burn!" or "Right thyself before fire purify thee." Jokes began to circulate around the campus about the professor having a scarlet letter "A" carved on his backside. Tolerance for his notes was growing thinner, and patience was running out. Everyone was saying (under their breath) that a day of reckoning was going to come to the professor for his notes.

And come it did. One night while he was burning the midnight oil, presumably churning out a fresh batch of his malevolent missives, the midnight oil caught fire. Actually, it turned out to be an electrical fire that began within one of the walls of his office. In a few moments' time, the soldier of God's holiness found himself trapped in God's building by unwanted worldly fire.

According to the story, both ends of that wing of the seminary burned up along the hallways and into the middle, where the professor and his office were located. By the morning, the firemen had begun to sift through the remains. They discovered the body of the professor beneath a huge wooden bookcase that had fallen away from the wall. Melted to his hand was his ever-present red sharpie marker. Beneath his desk was a stack of the brown leather notebooks in which he scrawled his messages.

As the fire hoses sprayed down the walls of the room, those who say they were present reported a most disturbing sight. When the soot and ash began to run slowly down the walls, dark streaks burned into the wall became apparent. In fact, it became obvious that these streaks were ridges, very much like the kind you make with a wood-burning kit.

These streaks were actually ruts burned into the walls, and they would never wash away. These streaks were forming letters. The letters formed words. The words formed a familiar Bible verse that wrapped around two walls. Burned into the wall of the professor's office in large letters measuring four feet high were the words "The greatest of these is love."

The sight of this unlikely fire coincidence unnerved the firefighting team and the policemen. They were left baffled and dazed, without any explanation as to how such a phenomenon was possible. Many felt it must have been an act of God to vindicate his good pleasure with the college and its spiritual labors.

The staff members, however, formed a different opinion about the astounding revelation. Most of them felt the fire must have been God purging the institution of a hostile old curmudgeon. Many a student chapel service prayer offered "thanksgiving for cleansing and protecting the school from hostility and disunity."

Within a year's time, the tale was retold that God wrote the words on the wall with his very own finger just like the Ten Commandments. It was said that the outcome of the event was a glowing endorsement of the university and proof that God was to be found in every little detail of every life event that happens.

The walls have long since been repaired and repainted. The strange letters that carved themselves into the sheetrock are covered up. With students rotating out every few years and a high level of staff turnover, the secret within the walls lies forgotten.

But if those walls could talk, who knows what other supernatural manifestations might yet come forth? Or more importantly, how would they be interpreted by the faithful?

CHAPTER 3

THE BLOODIEST FIVE HUNDRED YARDS IN AMERICA

If we think about highly charged emotional moments having the potential of leaving residual energy or ghosts behind, I should warn you that the Springfield town square has to be some five hundred of the bloodiest square yards in America.

There were three famous—or perhaps more correctly, *infamous*—events that took place on this soil. They are commemorated by historic markers in the square. But there was also a fourth that is mostly forgotten today, and yet, it was very instrumental in shaping Springfield's present reality.

It was October 1861 when the Battle of Springfield broke out. Union and Confederate soldiers clashed on this ground in three surges of attacks that lasted all through that long, long day. Over two hundred people were dead by the time the fighting ceased. The second Battle of Springfield was on January 8, 1863. Once again, these former friends, families and neighbors lined up across these streets to murder one another, and this time, the body count of wounded, missing and dead was around six hundred people. This battle featured some of the most horrific elements of the Civil War. There was hand-to-hand fighting, which was carried out from house to house through formerly quiet neighborhoods. This brutality led to the burning of civilian homes throughout the seemingly endless waves of attacks.

The Civil War is a huge source of ghost stories and the origin of many haunted places due to the close and personal nature of the conflict and the fact that everyone lost someone in that war. Photographer Matthew Brady brought the horrors of war home for the first time through his shocking

This fountain and sculpture greet you as you enter the Springfield town square. Although a tourist stop and popular gathering place for young people today, it has on many occasions been the location of severe violence.

These large displays mark the Battle of Springfield Civil War locations. This is the biggest historical marker in the square.

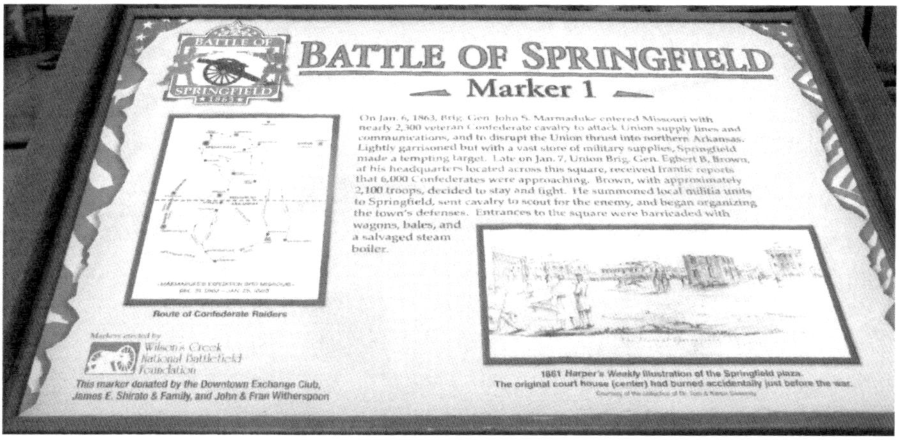

This is the marker that describes the first Battle of Springfield. The town is very proud of its Civil War history.

photos. This was the first time we could all see images of people we may very well know lying on fields, bloated, bloody and dead. Consequently, the Civil War is the haunting memory of a time when people were bent on violence to win their cause. It has left a deep and abiding scar on our nation.

On July 21, 1865, just a few years since the dead of the Civil War battles were cleared from this square, another incident occurred that is a study in the worst side of human nature and the almost mystical power of violence.

Wild Bill Hickok had been a Union scout during the Civil War, and the man he would murder on a corner in the Springfield square, Davis Tutt, had been a Confederate soldier. Tutt left his home in Arkansas to get away from a feud called the Tutt-Everett affair, in which several of his family members were killed. He wandered into Missouri to leave the violence behind. Hickok arrived in Missouri after thinking he had killed a man in a drunken brawl. Both of these tired warriors ended up in downtown Springfield.

Now, the stories that surround this shootout include allegations that Bill fathered a child with Tutt's girlfriend and that Tutt was making time with Bill's girl, too. The cold hard facts are that Wild Bill was in a card game at the Lyon House hotel, and Tutt was bankrolling other players in an effort to ruin Bill. In the end, Tutt's "expert" coaching of the players he funded enabled Wild Bill to walk away with nearly $3,000. Tutt was very angry and began to badger Bill. They started to argue over past card game debts, debating whether the amount owed was $35 or $25. To settle this discrepancy, Tutt grabbed up Bill's gold pocket watch off the table and announced to the crowd that he would keep it as collateral until he received another ten dollars. This embarrassment was one of the little things that made Bill "wild"!

When Tutt left the room, I wonder if he knew he was holding a watch that would mark how much time he had to live? In the coming days, Tutt and his cohorts teased Wild Bill about the watch and how great it looked on Tutt. One day, Bill was told that Tutt planned to wear the watch on a brand-new vest out in the town square. Wild Bill sent a message back to him that said not to wear the watch outside unless dead men can walk. Bill then went home to clean, oil and load his guns.

The next morning, Tutt walked out into the square with Bill's watch chain shining in the sunlight. Bill marched out to him, and much to everyone's surprise, the only shots that followed were the ones the two men threw back in a nearby bar. Apparently, they settled the issue and reached some kind of agreement for Bill to pay off the watch in a few days.

But at about 6:00 p.m. that same day, Davis Tutt waltzed back out into the square swinging Bill's watch. This time, angry and drunk, Bill pulled out

This is the street corner of the square where Wild Bill Hickok stood when he shot down Davis Tutt. Today, the adjacent building is the "History on the Square" museum.

his Colt pistol and stormed past the people on the sidewalks. Seeing the gun drawn and ready, the townspeople scattered inside for cover. "Here I am!" yelled Bill. Tutt stopped in his tracks, and the two men squared off almost exactly seventy-five yards apart. Wild Bill cocked his gun and lowered it back into his holster. Tutt did the same, and in one of the historic shootouts that went just like we have all seen in the movies, the two men stood sideways and stared each other down.

Suddenly, Tutt reached and pulled out his weapon, while Bill pulled his gun and steadied it on his other arm. Reports vary, but shots rang out almost simultaneously. Tutt missed Hickok. Hickok's shot ripped into Tutt's chest cavity between his fifth and sixth ribs. Slowly, he lowered his gun. He turned to face his friends and called out, "I am killed, boys," and he slumped to the ground, dead.

The shootout happened, and that might have been the end of that, but sometimes fate can be crueler than anyone can imagine. Here's an example. A man named George Nichols wrote a very stylized account of the shootout in *Harper's Magazine*, and its many exaggerations created the fame and legend of Wild Bill as a man who had killed hundreds of men. This grand reputation made Bill famous for his alleged penchant for violence. It made him a Wild West rock star. And Bill reaped the benefits of that star status. But it also made him a target for other tough guys out to prove they could best Wild Bill.

And, in fact Wild Bill's wild ride came to an end on August 2, 1876, in a place ironically called Deadwood. Deadwood was a most inelegant town in South Dakota. Bill was playing poker, and for the first time in his life, he did not sit with his back to the wall. Instead, oddly, he sat with his back to a door, and not one player at the table would change places with him, despite several requests.

A man named Jack McColl (better known to his friends as "Broken Nose Jack") walked in quietly behind Hickok, pulled his gun and yelled, "Damn you! Take that!" and fired point-blank into Wild Bill's head. The bullet passed out of his cheek and struck another player in the wrist. Bill slumped forward over his cards and bled out on the table.

So just what is Wild Bill's legacy? Some dead bodies; some old west folklore; at least a couple diseases, including quite possibly venereal disease; a restless haunted life; and the dead man's hand. That's the hand of cards Wild Bill was holding at the moment he died. Two eights, two aces, all black and one indifferent card newly dealt and not turned over yet.

The Civil War battles and the Wild Bill shootout were sensational events that have historic markers here on the square. There was another very violent incident that took place right here in the square that made national headlines because it shocked the entire world. It was April 13, Good Friday of 1906, the start of the Holy Day weekend. A white woman who was estranged from her husband was out on the town with another man. Allegedly, they were stopped and the woman "violated" by two black men.

A few hours later, Fred Coker and Horace Duncan, who had just finished work shifts at a nearby freight house, were arrested and thrown in jail as the chief suspects. The available evidence seemed to point to their innocence, but on Saturday night, an angry mob formed, fueled by stories of the wicked deeds of the two black men. This mob is estimated (depending on which report you believe) as being anywhere from four hundred to seven thousand people.

The mob stormed the jailhouse, and the officers inside handed the two men over to the rioters. They marched the men down to the town square, put ropes around their necks and hanged them over the bandstand railing of the Gotfried tower. The Gotfried tower stood right in the center of the square. It was a metal scaffold tower, all decorated with signage and buntings. Above the performance area of the bandstand stood a replica of the Statue of Liberty. From the railing of this bandstand now dangled the two dead bodies of Fred Coker and Horace Duncan.

But the sight of their homegrown vigilante justice did not satisfy members of this mob. They covered the two bodies in coal oil, and a bonfire was started beneath them. As the crowd cheered, the flames eventually consumed the flesh of these men and burned through the ropes dropping them into the fire below. But the sight, sound and smell of vigilante justice did not satisfy this mob. They knew that another black man sat in the jail. He was a young man named Will Allen, and he had been accused of killing a white man near Drury University. That was good enough for them. The mob returned to the jail, and the officers handed over this prisoner as well.

Allen was marched past the cremation fire and on to the bandstand. A rope was tied around his neck and then to the bandstand railing. He was given a mock trial, found guilty and shoved over the rail. But the jolt from the drop snapped the rope, and he fell into the bonfire below, causing a tower of flames to rise up.

This did not satisfy this mob either. They dragged his body out of the fire, hanged him again and cheered loudly when the flaming corpse fell once again onto the pyre. The flames illuminated the smiling faces of the crazed leaders of the mob still gathered on the bandstand, as well as the Statue of Liberty.

This illustration depicts the murders that took place on the horrific night of the 1906 "Easter offering."

The next day, Easter Sunday of 1906, many of the townspeople made their way to church, still smelling of smoke. The wide-eyed Christian children who inquired about the smoldering mess at the foot of the tower were told it was an "Easter offering." In fact, one local businessman did quite well for himself selling collectible medals stamped with the image of the tower and the words "Easter Offering, April 15, 1906," and on the backside were the words: "Hanging of three niggers, Springfield, Missouri." This horrific event is marked by a commemorative plaque on the base of the artwork for the history of the square. The plaque is just a couple inches off the ground and does not face up to people's eyes.

If you find yourself in the Springfield town square, take a good look around and see how long it takes you to find the historic marker for the murder of these black men. Good luck in your search. As the result of all these variations of murder and hatred, you can understand why the Springfield square is a very haunted place. It is haunted by its past and, according to locals, haunted by the souls of those who suffered in this place.

Along the side of the walkway in the square rests the marker for the "big book of historic highlights" of the town square.

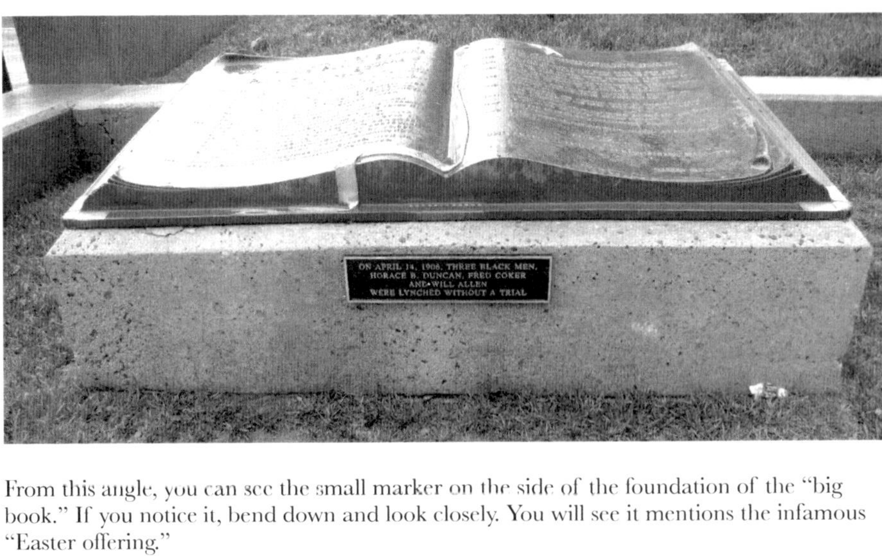

From this angle, you can see the small marker on the side of the foundation of the "big book." If you notice it, bend down and look closely. You will see it mentions the infamous "Easter offering."

And there it is, just the bare facts. When a representative of the NAACP came to town to recognize the "monument," she wept when she saw its content and placement.

A common ghostly experience here in Springfield is hearing the phantom sounds of the victims of these events. Some people have reported feeling warm or even hot as they passed through areas of the streets and hearing the actual sound of the flames of the bonfire, the shots of the gunfight and the cries of the wounded and dying of the battlefield. Be aware that standing in the square is standing on most unholy ground.

CHAPTER 4

THE PHANTOM LANDLORD OF JEFFERSON AVENUE

In the 1930s, the residential districts up and down Jefferson Avenue and its neighboring streets were mostly grand affairs. One of the ghost stories that arose from Springfield's little slice of suburban heaven has to do with one of those grand old houses. As best as we can figure, the original location of the house in this story was in the 1800 block of South Jefferson. Some of the persons involved in this tale still have family living and doing business here, so we will call them the "Smiths."

This big beautiful house was bought in 1939 by Mr. and Mrs. Smith. They had high hopes of filling its many rooms with children, and only two years later, Mrs. Smith was delighted to discover she was expecting. The couple was elated when she gave birth to twins, two fine sons to live in that big house with them. It was the beginning of the idyllic life they had always imagined.

But Christmas of that year was overshadowed by the fact that just twenty-two years after the end of the "war to end all wars," the Second World War began with the attack at Pearl Harbor. And, of course, like all able-bodied patriotic men, Mr. Smith, the head of this young household, enlisted in the armed services. Mrs. Smith did everything she could to be brave and tend to her family and aid the community on her own. She volunteered at her church and helped with metal and rubber drives for the war effort.

As Christmas rolled around again, one of the twins caught a fever and suddenly died. Before word reached the boy's father out in the field of battle, the other son tripped on a toy, tumbled down the big staircase in the front room and broke his neck. The grief-stricken mother waited for her

Most of the large old houses on Jefferson Avenue have been converted to apartments or offices.

husband to come home and ease her loss. But instead, she received a letter from the War Department. That letter explained to her in the best possible arrangement of eloquent words that her husband had been killed in battle and how much her country appreciated his sacrifice.

Winter hit harder that year than most here in Springfield, and this poor, shattered woman fell ill. Her neighbors happened to be a very kind and compassionate older couple who became worried when they noticed she hadn't been out of the house for days. They made some chicken soup, walked next door in the snow and wind and banged on the door. The door was unlocked, and it creaked and slowly swung open from the pressure of their knocking. It appeared that no one was home. The house was dark, it was cold and it was silent.

Slowly, the couple walked into the house, calling out and asking if anyone was home. They turned on lights as they went farther into the house. Eventually, they heard a faint, weak voice, and in an upstairs bedroom, they found her. She was lying in a bed covered with heavy comforters and old family quilts. She was shocking in appearance, gaunt, skeletal and barely alive. The man ran from the house to get a doctor while the woman stayed and offered what comfort she could.

The doctor told them it was a Christmas Eve miracle that they got help for her when they did, but still, he could not assure them she would pull through. He told them that he had given her medicine and she was resting comfortably but that she was literally at death's door. The loss of her husband and the tragedy of her twins had aged her well beyond her natural years. He suggested they check on her tomorrow and told them not to hesitate to summon him again if she was any worse.

The next day was a break in the terrible winter weather, and it was actually very pleasant and sunny outside. The worried neighbors were shocked to see the weary woman next door come out of her house, smiling, energetic and with a spring in her step. She was headed to their door. The man of the house couldn't help but wonder just what kind of medicine the good doctor had given her and if he might not benefit from a dose or two of it himself.

This revitalized woman was welcomed by the neighbors, who listened in amazement to the story of how she slept well for the first time in weeks because she had made a decision. She was going to rent out the rooms of her big house. This would solve her financial problems as well as her loneliness. It seemed that this decision had lifted all the weight of the world off her frail shoulders. She seemed reborn, and from that day forward, this woman was a whirlwind of compassion, good deeds and cheer. She baked pies and cakes for the sick and feeble, she sold war bonds door to door and, most of all, she cared for the little children at her church. Each week she would hold them, rock them and dote on them. She became a second mother to them. She rented out six bedrooms of her big house. Finally, she had the family she had always longed for, and she cooked and cleaned for them and poured herself into them.

As the holidays rolled around again, the woman stopped in at her neighbors' house and gave them a small gift. It was a little box wrapped and tied in a perfect bow. She warned them not to open the box until Christmas. In fact, she made them promise, and they did. When Christmas morning finally arrived, the neighbors tore into the little box that had more than tormented their curiosity. Inside, they found a house key. At first they were puzzled but then assumed that this most generous woman was giving them her house as a Christmas present. They ran next door to refuse the gift as simply too much.

They knocked on the door, but no one answered. Muffled noises began to rise from inside the house, but there was no answer at the door. The couple pulled the key from the box and unlocked the door, and as they stepped inside, they beheld a most bizarre sight. The dinner table was set with all the best china and a full tea set, and on the table, an assortment of wilted, rotting food was covered in cobwebs, bugs and mice. When they flicked on the chandelier light, the vermin dispersed and revealed the woman—or what used to be the woman—sitting at the head of the table in her Sunday dress. She was now, in fact, a corpse in an advanced state of decay. The scene was terrifying, as was the smell.

It soon became clear that the muffled noises, which were growing louder, were coming from the bedrooms. The man called for the police, and the woman unlocked the tenants from their rooms one by one. No one really knew what to think or how to explain what had happened in that house on Jefferson Avenue. But when the police and the examiners filed their report, it stated that the woman had been dead, as best they could calculate, a year. Was the ghost of this woman interacting with the living world in tangible ways for a year? Did her determined spirit create a "hiccup" in the timeline of reality? There are no easy answers to this anomaly. And the moral of this story, of course, is that you never really know who is watching your kids at church.

The truth about the lovely lady on Jefferson Avenue stunned the entire town.

CHAPTER 5

BACKSTAGE CASANOVA'S FALL FROM GRACE

On the campus of Drury University stands the Mabee Center for the Performing Arts. In one world-class facility, the center houses three distinct performance spaces: the Lydy Arts Center, the O'Bannon Music Center and the Clara Thompson Hall. The Lydy Arts Center and O'Bannon Music Center were built in 1979 to bookend the original Clara Thompson Hall, which was erected in 1926 in honor of its namesake.

The plaque on the hall says it was "erected to the memory of Clara Louise Wallace Thompson by her loving foster parents Washington Irving Wallace and Louise Grosebeck Wallace." Back in 1888, Clara was a dedicated and promising young pianist who was brought from Lebanon, Missouri, to attend what was then known as the Drury Conservatory of Music. Mr. Wallace had been one of the original members of the Drury Board of Trustees.

The new portions of the facility were made possible by private funding from the George W. O'Bannon estate, the Richard Lydy estate and the Mabee Foundation. Now it has furthered countless students in the study and performance of music and the arts, and it is a showcase of which the university is justifiably proud.

One of the more commonly acknowledged ghost stories from Drury is the ghost in Clara Thompson Hall. The earliest reports of the now legendary ghostly piano music emanating from the hall date back to the 1950s. The tales, like most ghost stories, seem to come in waves. The number of people reporting the phenomenon will increase and then taper off. More contemporary reports of a phantom spirit playing the piano on the stage began around 1981. Most will tell you with a smile that it must be the ghost of Clara Thompson lingering on her beloved piano.

We discovered another much less famous story that runs through the darker side of Drury's past. According to one graduate of the class of 1990, there was a love story that ended in tragedy. It was a heartbreaking tragedy that some believe has caused two more ghosts to occupy the Mabee Center for the Performing Arts: two star-crossed students who apparently will never, ever graduate.

In 1980, a student named Rick, a slender good-looking fellow from the tiny town of West Plains, Missouri, was a real ladies' man around the campus. The only thing he spent more time on than his hair was hitting on women. Rick was a fine arts major with an emphasis on drama. According to those who remember him, he had an overemphasis on drama of all kinds.

Rick had flair. He was always the center of attention, and the attention he fought for the most was that of the ladies. Rick was not overly picky about his women, either. As the semester reached its halfway point, Rick is remembered as having made many girlfriends cry. He was a love 'em and leave 'em guy—until he put his moves on a young lady named Grace.

Grace was the physical embodiment of her name. She grew up in an upper-class family from Springfield. She was a gifted musician and an honor student, and she was both crazy beautiful and pure as the driven snow. Her family had sheltered her from most of life's hardships and realities. Grace was unprepared for the deceptive charm and calculating words of Drury's backstage Casanova.

Apparently, Rick first saw Grace at an audition for the spring musical production. He immediately set out to befriend her. As cruel fate would have it, both were cast in the production of *The Music Man*. Rick, ironically, was the worldly-wise con man Professor Harold Hill, and Grace seemed born and bred for her role as the town librarian Marian Paroo. As far as Rick was concerned, the play would make his conquest of Grace a sure thing.

The weeks went by, and the two became an item. They were never seen apart from each other. It is unclear if any fellow students tried to warn Grace about Rick and his reputation. Rick complimented Grace's natural talent and wonderful voice. He suggested they rehearse some scenes in private, and she gladly agreed. Most of the time, these exclusive rehearsals took place in the green room behind the stage.

As they ran the lines and sang the songs, Rick plied his charms, and the love scene led to the kissing, the kissing to making out and soon much more than what could be done in the school green room. Grace was ecstatic at her good fortune. She was going to school, doing well with her studies, felt good about the play and was in love with a charming young man. In her young and naïve mind, she envisioned Rick proposing to her and them living happily ever after.

No one is quite sure what happened next, though one person familiar with the story said that Grace went uninvited to Rick's dorm room and discovered him in bed with another girl. My primary source for the details of this story heard that two other girls met her at the end of a hallway between classes and showed her very graphic notes from Rick that they had been receiving for months. Regardless of how it happened, Grace was shattered to discover that this special young man had played her for a fool and was making sport of it before the rest of the student body.

She could not imagine how anyone could be so heartless and cold. For the first time in her young life, she felt real anger and rage. Sadly, instead of Grace's good swaying Rick from his evil ways, his avarice poisoned her soul. The very next day, Grace did something rather brilliant but criminal.

Into Rick's backpack, she stuffed a sexually provocative note, a note she knew he would find. It contained an invitation that she knew he would find irresistible. He had deceived her for sex, and now it was her turn. The note asked if he would like to be part of the Drury "mile-high club." It then directed him to meet her on the lighting catwalk over the stage in the theatre. Rick was distracted most of the day by the thought of sweet Grace getting feisty.

At 3:00 p.m., he came to the theater and discovered another note taped to the eye-level rung of the ladder that led to the catwalk. It said, "Come and get it." Halfway up the ladder, a second note read, "Come and try to find Grace." At the top of the stairs, he saw Grace dressed in shorts with boots and a tube top. It was very uncharacteristic for her, and this distracted Rick even more.

It distracted him from noticing that on the dry erase board behind the middle section of the catwalk where Grace stood was written in a descending row the words "Give Rick A Chance: Explain." The letters from top to bottom spelled Grace.

As Rick reached the middle of the catwalk, Grace pulled him close and said, "Let's wait until everyone is down there." She kissed him as a growing number of students were filing onto the stage below for rehearsals. Once the murmur of activity had grown, she parted from him and drew his attention to the dry erase board.

No one can be certain of exactly what transpired between the two, but soon their voices grew loud enough to upset the students below. As an audience formed beneath them and an instructor shouted for them to come down this instant, a shot rang out and an anguished groan was heard followed by Rick's body, which came crashing down on the park gazebo set piece from the play.

Grace had shot the young man in the crotch. When he hit the gazebo roof and tumbled to the floor of the stage, he was still alive. Rick was mortally wounded but still conscious.

There were screams as the teacher ordered everyone off the stage and out of the theater, and an assistant was sent to call for the police. The instructor looked up only to see one of his favorite students, Grace, staring down from the catwalk with a small gun in her hand.

The instructor began calling out for her to put the gun down and come off the catwalk. Grace began to laugh, and through her unsettling laughter, she began to sing the song from her scene with Rick, "Til There Was You." The last thing anyone could make out of her words was "Are you listening, Rick? I'm gonna sing to you forever in hell!" There were other choice words intermingled in her crazed rant, but that much was very clear.

As the police and ambulance flooded into the auditorium, a second shot rang out, echoing off the cement walls and metal railings of the theater fixtures. Emergency personnel came to Rick's assistance, but he died on the floor of the stage. Grace was already dead from the self-inflicted wound. Her body was retrieved from the edge of the catwalk. They also recovered the two notes Rick had brought up there from the ladder.

Within days, the blood was washed away from the stage, the gazebo was rebuilt and another talented pair replaced Grace and Rick in *The Music Man*, which opened just as scheduled ten days after the incident. But those among the cast knew there was something disturbing about watching the sly salesman working the simple townsfolk and the demure librarian who falls under his spell.

Something else disturbing remained behind after the play closed: the haunting and unmistakable strains of "Til There Was You" being hummed and sung by a beautiful female voice—a voice that was very familiar to the cast members as that of Marian the librarian. It was Grace.

Just where this singing was coming from no one could be sure. It seemed to move around the room as you tried to follow it. Those who were sensitive to such things were certain it was Grace singing her eternal song to Rick as promised.

These stories no doubt merged with the previous tales of ghostly piano music coming from Clara Thompson. Perhaps Clara even gave ethereal accompaniment to young Grace. They might as well enjoy the time; they have so much of it now.

And as for Rick, is he in hell listening to an unending reminder of his lust and shame? One cannot be sure of such things exactly, but we could say, from what we know of Rick, that if he went to heaven, he, like his *Music Man* character, "wouldn't know the territory!"

CHAPTER 6

THE SPRINGFIELD INNER SANCTUM

In the early 1900s, the railroad tracks divided North and South Springfield into two separate towns. North Springfield became known for its outstanding industrial, manufacturing and transportation operations. South Springfield was the more upscale of the two, with a reputation as a broad service and retail economy. South Springfield was regarded as the more socially acceptable place to live and offered better residential options. The two towns were at times very uneasy neighbors.

During the years before these two towns merged into one, there was a mysterious homicide or suicide involving a man known only as "the Captain." Was it homicide or suicide? You decide.

This shadowy Captain kept at least two apartments down by the railroad tracks. He rode the rails and was gone for long stretches of time before returning to one of his homes. No one was sure where he went, what his business was or why he was called "the Captain," other than the fact that he wore a ship captain's hat.

When he was in Springfield, he lived large. He would buy everyone drinks and give lavish gifts to people who performed favors for him. This included a multitude of the "women of ill-repute" who frequented the wrong side of the Springfield tracks. For all intents and purposes, he was a suspicious character. But he threw money around freely at a time when money was very hard to come by, so he was always welcomed and never questioned.

And then one day, an unexpected end came to the mysterious Captain. He was found dead on the floor of the larger of his two apartments with a bullet in his brain and a gun in his hand. A woman who claimed to be his wife brought the police to the scene of the crime. Once they had assembled in the room, she threw herself on his body and began to sob and cry out, "Oh darling, my precious darling, you did this and killed yourself. Why did you do this to yourself? No one else but you did this." Now, in the detective business, this is called "very unusual and not just a little bit suspicious."

Since the man could not tell his own story and the woman claiming to be "Mrs. Mysterious Captain" disappeared later on that same night, the case was left with the overly obvious circumstantial evidence and deemed a suicide. As for his two apartments, they were completely empty, void of anything except a simple wooden chair, two empty orange crates and a small pouch of incense from the Orient.

On his person at the time of his death, he had no identification, no money and no keys. The only distinguishing mark on his body was a tattoo of a pentagram, which was found on his back between his shoulder blades. What did this man do? Who was he? Where did his money come from? Why did he live in two places in the worst possible neighborhood? The only answers we may ever have come from one other question: for whom did he work?

The first time we heard the story of the Captain was only a few months ago, and by asking around in our network of ghost story trackers, we stumbled on a fascinating tale that parallels the time of the Captain. We think the two stories go together, although we can't prove it just yet.

Thanks to the staggering number of ghost-based TV shows, ghost hunting is en vogue right now, but it was not always so. In years gone by, you could bear significant social and religious consequences for showing an unhealthy interest in the departed. Most of the curious souls who did such things in the past did so under the guise of genealogical research. They would roam around cemeteries matching names and dates and taking photos. They would scour estate sales and antique stores and flea markets for discarded family photos or heirlooms that could be connected with known ghost stories. They were also commonly found in the memberships of "Antiquity Societies," collecting artifacts from historic incidents.

We are grateful to those who braved the slings and arrows of social mores to do the hard work of linking the material world with traces and tales of supernatural occurrences. Keep them in mind when you encounter self-styled "ghost experts" who are simply looking for the thrill of some cheap "boos."

In 1886, one year before the two cities would merge, there were many people with agendas, particularly wealthy people, jockeying into position to gain sway over the expanding city and its soon-to-be realigned

This is the old Masonic Temple where Mr. Bernstein called the first meeting of his infamous Council of Elders.

government. Some of those who wanted control joined together in specific groups. There were influential groups, including churches, fraternities and even secret societies like the Masonic Lodge looking to play a role in the city's growth.

In the early days of Greene County, the Masonic Lodge not only served as a social and fraternal club but also settled disputes and concerns for the brethren and sidestepped the court system entirely. In a sense, the lodge was its own city within the city. The lodge grew and gave birth to many branches and related orders including cryptic masonry, the Oddfellows, the Mystic Shrine, Order of the Eastern Star, the Pleiades shrine, the Woodmen of the World and other bizarre-sounding sister organizations. Some of the splinter groups that arose from the lodge were forced to depart from lodge affiliation, as they were a just a little too strange, a little too serious and a little too far toward the occult.

Now, before we go any further, let us discuss this word "occult." It is a word that raises red flags, and to most people, it smacks of evil and Satanism. However, the actual word *occult* is a Latin term that simply means "hidden knowledge." This could be knowledge that is obscure and hard to find, and it can refer to knowledge that is being kept away from the general public for a specific purpose, although it usually it refers to a search for the deeper, more spiritual reasons or meanings behind life and the universe.

So in the simplest of terms, the actual recipe for Kentucky Fried Chicken is occult knowledge, as would be the knowledge of how to channel unseen power and spiritual energy—that is, of course, if the desired information exists in the first place.

Out of the Springfield lodge organization came a group of men devoted to the idea that they could and should influence the future of the city. In fact, they apparently felt they should take control of the city and direct its affairs almost completely. The earliest known record of this group reveals that its founder's name is Mr. Franklin Bernstein. Mr. Bernstein published an announcement for the initial meeting of "The Council of the Elders" on a handbill distributed to members of the lodge in April of that year.

As unbelievable as it may sound, the group seems to have been dedicated to the study and pursuit of controlling others through occult rituals. The Council of the Elders, as best as we can reconstruct, was expelled from associating with the Masonic Lodge soon after its first meeting. Now, on a practical level, one might interpret losing the support of your fraternal friends as a blow to the idea that you can bring everyone under your control. But hey, people still look for Bigfoot too, right?

It appears that after some months and a few false starts, Mr. Bernstein and three others finally formed an organization that was renamed simply "the Elders." They met privately in the homes of the participants. One of these four men has a surviving relative in Joplin, Missouri. He is the source of most of the narrative we are about to share with you.

The Elders embraced the idea that others could be persuaded by unseen spiritual forces that they would command through incantations, rituals and a homegrown form of voodoo. The Elders cast spells on the leaders of the township in an effort to force them into what they called "A Monkey's Paw Quandary." The monkey's paw is a concept that has been around for ages and was the foundation for the famous short story of the same published in England in 1902 by author W.W. Jacobs.

In this brilliant short story, a couple comes into possession of an enchanted monkey's paw. They are told it will grant them three wishes. They wish for a large amount of money to pay off their house so they can live free from that major expense. They soon discover they are receiving a large amount of money, more money than they had ever hoped for. But they soon learn the money was from a settlement because their son had been mangled and killed in an industrial machinery accident.

The boy's mother becomes stricken with grief. She takes up the monkey's paw and wishes that her son would return from the dead. Soon a knock is heard at the door, but the father, who identified his son's body after the accident, knows his appearance will be far too grotesque for his wife to bear. So quickly, he makes the third wish, and the knocking stops.

The premise is that the monkey's paw can grant wishes. The problem is that the granting of the wish carries with it an unforeseen moral consequence from which there is no pleasant way out. This is what the Elders had in store for North and South Springfield's leadership. They each practiced their dark rituals in the hopes of creating a crisis that only they could solve. And solving the dilemma would allow them to take up positions of authority and wealth.

One member of the Elders was a highly specialized surgeon. He befriended those in power so that if their health were threatened, they would naturally turn to him for help. In their moment of need, he would control their fate.

Another Elder was a powerful lawyer, and he plotted to ruin the reputation of those the Elders cast their hexes on. The plan was for these leaders to fall into questionable and suspicious circumstances. Then, the lawyer would destroy their moral credibility and force them to carry out the Elders' decisions.

The third man was the principal of South Springfield's private school. He set his nefarious efforts on charting the whereabouts and habits of the children of the city's leaders. Like Mr. Bernstein, he was independently wealthy and believed by many to be the man who bankrolled the mysterious Captain. The connection between Mr. Bernstein, the Elders and the Captain appears to revolve around any number of illegal items being imported at great cost. It is suspected that the Captain used the railroads to import many shipments of contraband, including drugs, and some of the more exotic items used by the Elders in their ceremonies, including their divination map, a large square of cloth that has been soaked in substances like various dyes, incense compounds and possibly even blood.

The cloth had drawings common to such devices. It would have words like "yes" and "no" inscribed on it, as well as pictures of a hand, a pentagram, mystic numbers and so forth. You can think of it as the placemat of the damned. And upon this cloth, the Elders would place specially colored candles, burn incense and arrange talismans or fetishes. These objects could be used to represent the people on whom they were casting spells.

We have been told that when initial efforts to swing the universe in their direction failed, the Elders eventually adopted another tactic. They simply decided to curse everyone, and to do it, they joined together in a marathon

Strangely enough, the old Masonic Temple is right next door to the Landers Theatre.

session of ritual dark magic. They summoned up all the restless spirits of the dead to drive men to madness, women to wreck their own marriages and to stir up every form of crime and chaos in the city. If they couldn't have the city of Springfield, it would forever more be a place tormented by specters, ghosts, malevolent spirits and boogeymen of every sort.

Ironically for men who sought to work a monkey's paw quandary on their fellow man, they seem to have merely forged a monkey's paw deal with the devil. We are told that the members of the Elders group came to disastrous ends. Each of these evil, greedy men fell prey to their own desires and devices—shockingly true to the monkey's paw story.

The surgeon suffered a nasty gash down the back of his leg while coming down off a ladder outside of his house. The cut sliced into an artery that would require some immediate expert medical attention. However, being the only specialized surgeon in town and unable to operate on himself, he bled out and died while waiting for help in the hospital.

The school principal was killed when a basement steam room boiler exploded. He was reportedly standing on a small step stool between the boiler and a wall looking at the children out of a small window when the boiler exploded.

The lawyer was ruined professionally by rumors of illicit and deviant sexual behavior. These charges were made by some of Springfield's more famous women of ill repute, the ones who did business down near the railroad tracks. He left Springfield ashamed and penniless. Was this some form of revenge from the Captain's "wife" and her friends?

Lastly, Mr. Bernstein and all traces of his shadowy organization disappeared along with everything in the mysterious Captain's two apartments. It is a surviving relative of Mr. Bernstein who has shared this story with us.

Some ghost hunters believe that the city of Springfield is, in fact, crawling with the spirits unleashed by the efforts of the Elders. They also point out to me that only those who invoke the spirits can return them to rest. Since the Elders all died or vanished, could it be that the evil invisible forces that push the city will never end?

CHAPTER 7

ROUTE 66 AND THE HIGHWAY TO HELL

Ever been in a movie when that thing happens where the frame on screen locks up and then melts through until the screen is totally stark white? It's not as common as it used to be with the advent of digital formats, but it used to happen fairly often, followed by an awkward delay while the celluloid was spliced by the projectionist and restarted. If you have seen this phenomenon, have you ever wondered what caused it?

The official answer, of course, is that a worn, clunky bit of film has a damaged sprocket hole, and that little bit of bent, stretched or crumpled material throws the projector's threading system into chaos. The film pops out of alignment and sits too long in front of the lamp, where it melts through. That's a technical answer, but there was a time when some youth around Springfield believed in a much more frightening reason, a reason born out of America's own adolescent past.

In the 1950s, something happened that had never happened before. In the post–World War II economic boom, American teenagers were empowered with spending money, and they spent it on the things teenagers love the most: themselves.

This hedonistic streak, coupled with unexpected family prosperity, led to an unprecedented rise in sales of cars, spiffy new cars that could be filled with gasoline and hormones. Teens with cars need special places to express their youthful enthusiasm for one another. A capitalistic society is nothing if not accommodating to a new spending demographic, and so it came to pass that each town saw the rise of the drive-in movie theater, those magnificent bastions of culinary anomalies, promotional gimmickry and B-grade cinematic fare. Drive-in movie theaters suddenly dotted the landscape of America's heartland.

Add to this formula of expendable cash, the drive-in movie and the age-old desire of youth to break free and go their own way one of Springfield's most famous historic attractions: Route 66. This famous highway across America represented the way out. It was a path to glorious freedom.

The story we share with you now brings these elements together. If you were young and had dreams of finding love and leaving town, Route 66 whispered promises of a better future, but in some cases, it became a highway to hell.

The Sunset Drive-In opened in the spring of 1950. It was located on the West Chestnut Expressway, right on Route 66. The "Sunsetter," as it came to be called, was a very popular spot for the newly mobile teenagers. It was not only a place for entertainment but also an important hub of social notoriety for the high school students. Being seen there and with whom became talking points for gossip and chitchat at school. During football season, the drive-in became a place to express rivalries. Egging cars belonging to the other team's players and even dragging someone out of his car for a "pantsing" was not uncommon. Such was the world of the Springfield teen in the 1950s.

Our story begins in 1957. Two students from Springfield's Central High School, the oldest high school in town, found each other in the cafeteria one day and immediately fell in "teen love." No doubt they felt Elvis was singing "All Shook Up" just for them, or if they were from less hip families, it was most likely Johnny Mathis's "Chances Are." Regardless of what their favorite song was, these two, whom we will call James and Virginia, were living the teen experience to its fullest. And that's when the trouble started, trouble that would lead to a horrifying end neither of them could have imagined.

The pair had been dating for a couple months when they unexpectedly received a parental "chewing out" by Virginia's folks for staying out an hour past the previously agreed on curfew. Her parents also made it clear that they felt the two were spending too much time together. The parents carefully worded their complaint that way since the original statement that they saw too much of each other seemed too morally frightening when said out loud.

This oppression seemed too much to bear. And although what her parents actually asked for was simply that they please observe the curfew and spend their date time in more open, social places around other people, it felt to the couple as if some intruder was sucking the spark from their young love.

James resented the conversation and a week later suggested to Virginia that they up and run away. They could pack their clothes, grab the family car and some cash and head that big Chevy down Route 66. They would leave their troubles and the old people behind to regret having ever been so unkind toward them. They talked with great enthusiasm about the life they would begin together in a new town. They fantasized about the future, and it gave them hope and a plucky confidence. It also gave them a secret to share. That is all very exciting stuff for teenagers in love.

Needless to say, the secret plan slowly leaked out to some of the other students at school, and everyone was watching to see James and Virginia blaze the trail of emancipation. Why, if they can do it, then it's possible for everyone else! A date was set for the last Friday of the month, two weeks away.

Unfortunately, as these two weeks passed, James began to realize that talking about running away and actually doing it were two very different things. They both admitted that the world would not be a friendly place for two roaming teens in a stolen car. They also carefully calculated that they would run out of money in three days. The more they discussed the details of their escape, the more they saw that it simply could not work.

When the day of their scheduled departure came, they showed up at school, as usual, right on time. And as is the habit of high school students, the other teens quickly began to mock and ridicule the couple. In the end, they were all talk and no action, and the kids at school were merciless in their teasing. Despondent over the loss of his shining vision of freedom and self-will, James fell into a serious teenage depression, and Virginia did her best to console him.

To make matters even worse, James discovered that his parents had caught wind of their plan to run away from home. Consequently, he was stripped of his privileges, including use of the family car and seeing Virginia. He was grounded for a month.

Now the two only saw each other at school. James became a constant concern to Virginia, who was worried that he was so depressed he may try something desperate. If only she could think of something to lift his spirits and stop the ridicule of the other students! Soon, an idea began to take root in her mind. It's not a new idea, but it seemed like just the thing to remedy this dire teenage situation.

She knew that his month of punishment at home would be over in another week, and she also knew just what would put the life back in her downtrodden young hero. Her efforts to encourage James now took the form of a promise of "going all the way" at the drive-in movie theater.

That's right, Virginia's plan was for their first date in a month to be defiant toward parents, make a legend out of James and stop the teasing of the other students once and for all. It would be the most sensational, scandalous thing that ever happened. And as young ladies often do, she felt certain this deed would make sure that her relationship to James would last forever.

Needless to say, James came out of his depression almost immediately upon hearing Virginia whisper in his ear what she had in store for him. They both began to fantasize about the Friday night that was fast approaching. They also remembered to casually, purposefully, inadvertently let it slip out during class. James just happened to mention it to some guys during his gym class. And he may have said something during his math and his biology classes. Virginia did the same. By the time the final bell rang at 3:00 p.m. on Friday, the couple was getting whoops and hollers and giggles from their classmates as they made their way down the hall and out the front door of the school.

Just as scheduled, James picked Virginia up right on time for their date with destiny. Both sets of parents were ironically very supportive of them going out and seemed genuinely happy that the two of them were together again. With parental blessings and an unexpected additional five-dollar bill slipped into his hand by Virginia's father, the two made their way to the "Sunsetter." They made sure they parked away from the other cars, near the back corner wall by the dumpsters. This decision was one of several they would come to regret.

It was a double feature that night in Springfield: a ridiculous science fiction film called *The Deadly Mantis* followed by *The Delinquents*, a film by a very young Robert Altman about troubled youth. As the couple began their journey through the first of the double features, they quickly shifted their attention from the popcorn to each other. They transitioned from awkward to aggressive. Soon, the front seat of the car was serving merely as a rack for discarded clothing and the back seat as the worst cheap hotel room in recorded history.

Just as the night was fulfilling its promise, an unwelcome intrusion shattered the young lovers' passion. The car began to bounce up and down from the weight of someone jumping on its rear bumper. Startled, the couple looked up and out of the half steamed-up rear window. Outside the car, yelling and banging on the body, James saw four big guys from his gym class. These were not his friends. They were two-bit hoodlums.

No one can be totally sure about exactly what happened next, but we do know that the boys broke out the driver's-side window using the movie speaker device, let themselves into the car, dragged a naked James out onto the gravel and mercilessly beat him senseless. Two of the boys picked him up and put him in the trunk of the car.

From his dark prison in the trunk, he could hear them each abusing Virginia in the back seat. James screamed over and over again, and he pounded on the trunk and made a frenzied effort to find a way out and rescue her, but alas, he could not.

In one moment, James and Virginia screamed together, albeit in a far different manner from what they had anticipated. At this precise moment, three things happened. First, the frame of film on the movie screen froze and then melted to a blank screen. Second, Virginia died when one of the boys strangled her with her own stockings. And finally, James fell unconscious in the trunk, and before the movie was over, he died as well.

Long after the drive-in lot had cleared out, the clean-up crew discovered the car and its grisly contents. The strange case of the murdered teenage lovers scandalized the town and drew fresh attention to the growing "youth problem" along Route 66. Springfield hosted a town meeting, hoping to get clues that would lead to an arrest, but no arrest was ever made in the case. The school began to emphasize safety and chastity to its students.

But the story is far from over. From that day forward, it seems that the ghosts of this pair of amorous teens began to torment and disturb other teens that came to this same drive-in to pursue unbridled passion. Many a young lady reported feeling a strange presence or a bizarre freezing cold temperature during an otherwise-heated car adventure. These young women say they got the sense of being warned not to continue and to return home and listen to their parents.

Even more remarkable, many young men reported seeing the ghostly visage of a brutally beaten boy with a huge gash down the side of his head looking in through the car windows at them or sometimes appearing inside the car with them. These terrifying experiences took a major toll on how much teenage hanky-panky went on at the "Sunsetter," and the number of couples finding their thrill on Blueberry Hill dropped dramatically.

Over the years, the tales of these ghosts disappeared along with the drive-in theaters and that golden period of American teenage history. Some say the apparitions ended when the four boys who committed the murders died of VD. Other versions of the story say that James and Virginia's entire class perished in a freak school bus accident. Apparently, the driver swerved to miss two naked teenagers who appeared directly in front of him as the bus passed the drive-in.

The Sunset Drive-In is long gone now. In its place stands a trailer park. The theater survived a tornado but could not withstand the onslaught of television and home video. But some people from Springfield say these battered ghosts will still appear in your headlights when you pass through Springfield on the old path of Route 66.

CHAPTER 8

TALES FROM THE OLD FOLKS' HOME

In the course of preparing this book, we held open meetings in several types of locations. We collected ghost stories from people everywhere, from dark corners of pubs to street corners full of hipsters to homes and places of business. The most fascinating, however, turned out to be one of the most unexpected, albeit logical locations: retirement communities.

Yes, here were groups of people who had lived full lifetimes. They represented every imaginable sector of society. There were war heroes, schoolteachers, celebrated entertainers and musicians, engineers, truck drivers, salesmen, writers and all stops in between. These diverse individuals had only two things in common: one, they were now living in a retirement community, and two, they all had ghost stories.

These remarkable folks told us chilling tales from their long lifetimes of experience. Some of these stories are found in other parts of this book, but here in this section we report to you the most bizarre and compelling tales from the old folks' home. Pull your shawl around your shoulders, and settle into your rocking chair. It's going to be a wild ride.

DEAD ROVER, DEAD ROVER

One gentleman well into his nineties waited until the end of one of our storytelling sessions to relate his experience. After the room had emptied of others, he told us of a strange experience that had begun six years ago and continues to this very day.

He recounted to us that back in 1992, he bought his wife a dog for their fiftieth wedding anniversary. She loved that dog so much he used to tell people he was afraid she loved the dog more than she did him. And anytime he said that in front of other people, she would press down on his knee and say, "Oh, Charles!" It became another little affectionate game in their life together.

Another little game they played involved the dog directly. In the morning, the little dog would eventually try to wake them up. Some days they would hurry and get up and talk to the dog in a way that got him very excited. The dog would run around the house and back to them several times in a rush to start the day. Other times they would ignore the dog. This caused the frustrated canine to attempt more and more outrageous tactics to rouse his humans. His favorite tactic was to bite the sheet hanging off the side of the bed and pull and pull and pull until it came loose from the foot of the bed. The couple would laugh and laugh at the tenacity of their pet and eventually get up, tuck the sheet back in and go on with the day.

But as time eventually defeats us all, the idyllic life of this couple and their furry companion was shattered when the woman fell ill and died in 2003. She was mourned by her family, her church and, most of all, by her faithful husband, who now felt lost, alone and angry.

Life went on, but nothing was ever the same. He said that loneliness and bitterness nearly killed him. He resented every day that started with the awareness that his love was missing from their bed and their home. Oddly, he began to project this anger toward the little dog that had been his gift to her.

Each morning, the dog would faithfully try to wake up his master in his familiar playful way. But now the man would, at best, ignore the animal, and at worst, he began to shove it off the bed or hit it. And sometimes he hit the little dog way too hard.

As his depression grew worse, his abusive behavior toward the dog grew worse, too. He would tease, torment or outright hurt the dog. But dogs love their people unconditionally, and the little fella continued to try to please and engage his master. Each day, he would tug the sheet loose from the foot of the bed, and each day, this act of affection was met with a swift kick that caused a yelp and a quick retreat under the dining room table to hide.

Finally, the man had enough of this living reminder of his wife. He took the dog on a walk from which he knew it would never return. He walked the dog out of their neighborhood and across a wooded field to a roadside gas station, isolated from everything but the highway. Once behind the gas station, he took the leash and collar off the unsuspecting pet, dropped a fistful of treats on the ground and briskly walked away.

At first, he felt smug and clever for what he had done, but that feeling slowly gave way to the realization that he had most certainly left this innocent creature to panic and face certain death from starvation, the highway or another animal. Now he felt shame and regret. He got out of bed extra early that morning and headed back to the area where he dropped off the dog, hoping now to rescue instead of abandon. Perhaps, he thought, there was still time to undo the evil he had done.

The journey back to the gas station seemed longer than before. The man was anxious to discover if he could save his forsaken companion. Sadly, he could find no sign of the dog, and his inquiries to the men inside the gas station provided no information or comfort. He walked slowly back home, calling the dog all along the way.

Now the sadness and depression of his wife's death was coupled with self-loathing and shame. He began to hate himself for doing such an unthinkable and inhumane deed. His thoughts tortured him with the idea that his blessed wife would despise the wicked, cruel man he had become. The whole affair drove him deeper into depression, which now took on the form of a determined wish for death.

After all, he thought, why did he deserve any better than what he had done to the little dog? He had abandoned the dog out of anger because his wife abandoned him, and he blamed God for all this loss and hurt. Once he arrived back home, he sat in his wife's favorite chair and stared out the window, lost in his despair.

By nighttime, he had made his plan to take his own life. He walked around the little house and straightened up his belongings. He left a simple note taped to the television for his daughter to find. It simply said, "I'm so sorry. I'm so tired. Forgive me. I'm going to be with your mother."

In the bathroom, he found the remains of three prescription medications his wife had taken, along with a bottle of over-the-counter sleeping pills. He spilled all the pills into his hand and washed them down with the last third of a bottle of whiskey. Then he lay down in his bed.

The sad little man began to drift in and out of consciousness, and the world around him began to melt and shift shapes in a terrifying series of drug-induced hallucinations. Much to his dismay and horror, he felt panic not peace. His senses were going wild, not fading quietly away. Finally, things did begin to slow down. His perception and his heartbeat began to slow. He felt cold and as if he were drifting away from his own body.

The corner bedsheet pulled out by a faithful canine companion—albeit, a betrayed and deceased companion.

Suddenly, he felt something else. This something else was coming from outside his body. It was a tugging. It was a steady rhythmic motion toward the end of the bed. Through the haze of his confusion, he sensed and then saw the end of the bedsheet pulled out and away from the end of the bed. It was sticking out in midair, being tugged over and over again. Eventually, the sheet came loose from the end of the bed and was pulled to the side onto the floor.

Was he imagining this? Was it the last delusions of a dying old man? Or was it something else? It suddenly gripped his confused mind that this was the ghost of his little dog, doing what he had always done. The dog was trying to get him up out of bed, only this time it would be to save his life. The man sat up in bed and discovered he was looking straight into the photo on the dresser. It was the picture of his wife holding the dog. The tugging stopped, and the sheet dropped to the floor.

He stumbled out of bed and called for help, and after an overnight stay in the hospital, he came back home determined to live and forgive. Eventually, he left his home for the safety and security of the retirement community. The one thing that stayed the same was the faithful ghost dog waking him up by tugging the sheet. He said it still happens every day.

He told me this story with tears in his eyes and showed me the rumpled sheet pulled to the side of the bed in his room. While no one has ever captured photos or other hard evidence of the spirited pooch, the sincerity of the storyteller is beyond doubt. Perhaps dog is man's best friend forever.

THE BEAUTIFUL MUSIC MY MOTHER PLAYED

This story was related to me by a senior citizen who resided in a particular retirement community in Springfield. She has been living there for nearly a decade and, in that time, has seen many people come and go.

She has seen the flashing red lights of the emergency vehicles shining through her bedroom window hundreds of times. Each time she sees it, she knows that someone she sees every day—perhaps someone she played bingo with or ate supper with—may be sick, injured or dying. She told me that each time that stretcher rolls someone out of the building, she just feels sick. She is sad for the trouble another human being is having and sad and troubled over her own best friend who died in the building seven years ago. She says this friend never left the building.

The friend in question was a resident named Mary Anne. Now, that is not her real name out of sensitivity to her surviving family, but it's close enough for our purpose of recounting this fantastic tale.

Mary Anne used to participate in many of the community's daily activities. She was a regular at bingo, card games and movie nights. She always went on every bus trip. Mary Anne delighted the others with tales of her childhood. She would tell hilarious stories of growing up in Springfield and sweet, heartwarming stories about her mother.

Mary Anne related so many stories about her beloved mother that many of the other residents and staff started to feel like they knew her, too. The favorite story was about how Mary Anne absolutely loved to listen to her mother play the piano. On Sunday afternoons after church, her mother would invite her to stand beside the piano in their living room and listen to her play. She played lovely hymns, show tunes and, if the mood hit her just right, even some boogie-woogie.

As her mother played, little Mary Anne would rest her head against the top of the piano and just drink in every aspect of the experience, like her mother's angelic countenance, the peacefulness of her home and how everything seemed right with the world as long as the music flowed. So vivid were the descriptions and memories she shared that everyone was saddened to discover that Mary Anne had been diagnosed with dementia. It seemed the most precious things she had were her memories, and now they would begin to slip away from her.

As expected, her tales began to drift, and her memories became jumbled, along with her ability to communicate them. They all faded except for the memory of her mother at the piano. At a certain point, she began to sit in one of the lobby chairs and face a painting on the wall. I'm told that it was a painting of a nice-looking woman in a dress playing the piano. Mary Anne began to invite people to sit by her and "watch Mother play," and some did. As her mind grew weaker, her friends grew stronger for her. They did sit. They sat for hours and watched Mother play.

On one occasion, Mary Anne was found by the staff in the wee hours of the morning sitting in that chair, apparently conversing with her mother via the woman in the painting. This went on for several weeks until she became sick with pneumonia. During that time, she had to stay in her room for several days.

It was on a Tuesday that one of the staff brought the woman telling me this story a note from her friend Mary Anne. She opened the note at the dining room table, where she was seated with several ladies who were all friends. The note said, "My mother says you're all invited to come to hear her play the piano on Sunday afternoon. I will need my good dress."

The eyes of the ladies at the table watered as they thought about this poor woman. They all agreed that they would make an effort to see her on Sunday if she was well enough for visitors. When Sunday came, so did an ambulance and a crew of emergency medical workers. They rushed through the front doors and into the elevator.

Those in the lobby and dining room gathered around, hoping to find out who was in jeopardy. Word slowly drifted among the residents that it was someone on the third floor. In a few more minutes, it was common knowledge that the emergency was in Mary Anne's room. Another team of EMTs arrived on the scene and rushed to the room as well. After an hour's time, the second team of helpers was seen leaving the building and driving away.

Shortly after that, the dreaded but familiar sight of a covered stretcher transporting the body of a newly departed resident rolled through the lobby and out to the ambulance. The woman who told me this story said she burst out into tears knowing that dear, sweet lady was gone. Perhaps, she thought, Mary Anne really will be with her blessed mother today in heaven.

It was at that exact moment that she saw something she had never seen before. So startling was this new awareness that it took her breath away, and she had to sit down. Now sitting in the chair Mary Anne had sat in for so many hours, looking right at the painting of the woman at the piano, she saw something new. If not new, then it was something she could not believe she had missed over all this time.

Her eyes looked over the image carefully. There was the proper-looking woman sitting up at the piano, her hands on the keyboard and the top of the piano, but now there was also the image of a beautiful little girl in a pretty dress resting her head on her arms on top of the piano. Was it possible? Could it be that Mary Anne joined her mother inside the image of the painting?

Logic and science tell us such a thing is not possible. Even the woman telling the story started out by claiming that what she was about to tell can't be real. But to this day stands a painting on the wall of a retirement community in Springfield, Missouri, that at least three witnesses will agree changed to include a little girl.

Was this a trick of tired minds suffering from emotional fatigue? Was it due to an oversight during previous viewings of the painting? Could it be that someone hung a mostly the same but partially different painting on that same wall overnight? Or did the spirit of this little girl manifest itself

Here is a close-up of the painting, showing the little girl looking lovingly at the woman playing the piano.

inside of a painting that, in her mind, was a place where she belonged? However slim the odds are that this could be true, if it is, then what are the other images in the paintings surrounding us every day? I now know the first questions I'm going to ask if I ever visit an art shop in the twilight zone!

The Watchman on the Bed

We will now share with you the shortest and most direct ghost story we have ever been told. We will give it to you as a direct transcript of the recording we made of a woman at the retirement community. I hope you appreciate the overt silliness of this story, as well as the sublimely horrific implications. Enjoy.

> *I have been haunted by my husband since the day he died back in 2009. He still makes his presence known to me and all my visitors. He is especially bothersome at night, when I have company in my room. We finally get ready*

to sleep, and you can feel this weight come down on the edge of the bed. It's him. I can tell it's him 'cause I recognize the shape of his butt. That has scared off every boyfriend I had for the last five years.

THE CHAIR AT THE END OF THE HALL

In these old folks' homes, there are almost always bits of furniture along the hallways. These provide a resting place for a fatigued resident or a place to sit and visit with a friend or neighbor. More often than not, these consist of upholstered chairs, the tall wing chairs that look like they came for a movie adaptation of a Charles Dickens novel or the kind a dreadful villain would sit in while dialoguing and groping the end of his walking cane. At one location, we were told a most terrifying story about a special visitor who used one of these chairs to watch and to wait. That visitor's name was death.

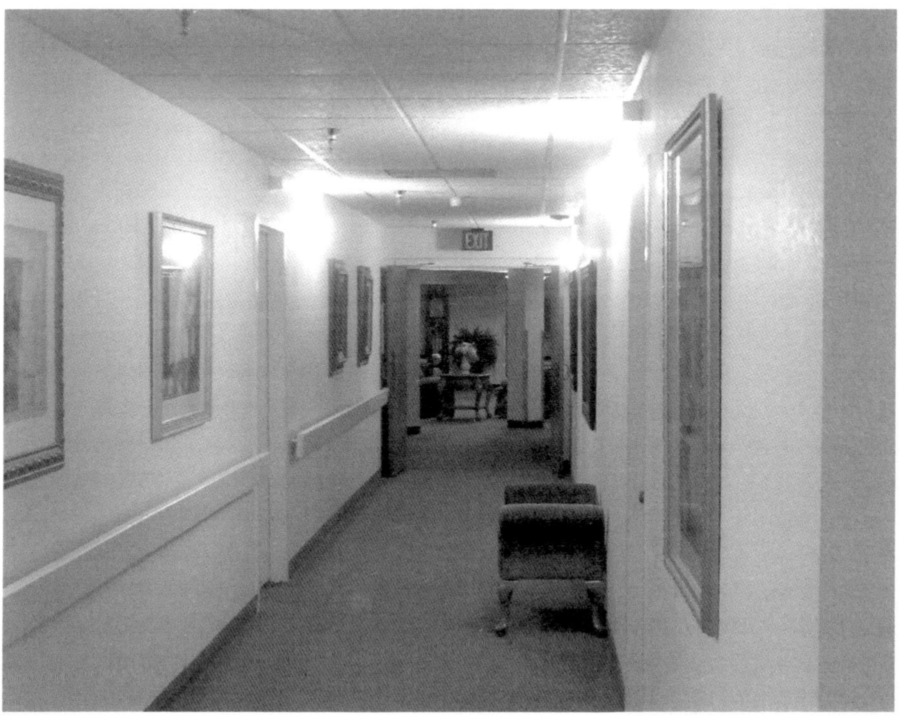

The endless maze of hallways and the resting places along them.

As we have already mentioned, the daily grind at a retirement home includes some unpleasant events. The most unpleasant of all is dealing with a resident who has just passed on. Sometimes the deceased is discovered by the staff in the morning. Sometimes they are not discovered for a day or two, and sometimes the death occurs while emergency medical workers are trying to save the person.

Inevitably, death comes to these facilities, the same way it comes to hospitals and private homes. Truly, it seems, at a specific moment in someone's life, death will not be denied. This sad fact is accepted by the residents of retirement communities. They know that each day at breakfast, the room may hold one fewer familiar face.

At one particular retirement home in Springfield, a man told us of his very strange experience. He said that he had just moved into an apartment within the home. He was still adjusting to the little one-bedroom living space after having been in a three-bedroom house for over forty years.

His first night in this new place was very restless. It just didn't feel like home, and he wondered if it ever would. Somewhere around three o'clock in the very early morning, he heard a thud and a crash. To him, it seemed to come from behind his bedroom wall. He assumed it was the bedroom of the apartment next to his. By the time he got out of his bed and into his robe and slippers, there were already emergency medical workers headed down the hall, carrying bulky shoulder bags and rolling a stretcher piled high with mysterious boxes and medical equipment.

He stepped outside to ask if the woman in the next apartment was alright. One of the medical personnel told him that she would be fine and to please go back to his room. He did step back but not into his room. Instead, he sat in one of those tall wing back chairs located at the end of the hallway. From there, he planned to watch to see what happened. Time dragged on, however, and the man dozed off right there in the chair.

The sound of the paramedics' radio getting another emergency call woke him up. He took off his glasses, rubbed his eyes and looked toward the woman's apartment. There was activity and discussion taking place, which became more noticeable as the door was propped open by one of the workers. About this time, his bleary eyes came back across the hallway, and he gasped as he saw, sitting in the chair directly across from the woman's apartment door, death. The Grim Reaper was just as he had seen in artwork and movies for many years. He had a long, lean build and was dressed in a black robe. There was a hood up and over the head, and nothing could be seen inside the hood—only blackness. In his skeleton hand was the winnowing blade. The man began to call out, but the hooded figure raised his boney finger to his invisible lips and gestured to quiet him. Too confused and afraid, the man did nothing but stare at this incomprehensible sight.

Then, as the murmur of activity increased by the apartment doorway, death stood up and walked through the doorway. Less than a second later, the man heard the heart monitor change to that dreaded steady tone. That is the unmistakable sound of a heart stopping. It was the sound of death. The robed figure stepped back out of the room with the ghost of the woman holding on to his wrist. They turned to the man and took a little bow. And with that arrogant deed, the grim reaper, with the woman's ghost, simply disappeared into thin air. The medical workers went into a frenzy to try and revive the woman, but it was all to no avail. Death had come to apartment 212.

Later in the day, the man tried to express what he had seen to others. This story was greeted with unbridled hostility. Needless to say, it did not help him make new friends in a strange place. Another old man suggested very loudly that he dreamed the whole thing while sitting in the hallway. That would be a logical explanation. He was tired after a stressful moving day, in unfamiliar surroundings. He saw the imposing sight of the paramedics and all that commotion. It didn't take long to convince himself that in fact he had dreamed the whole improbable thing. But then it happened again.

On this night about a week later, he was washing clothes in the laundry room. It was after ten o'clock at night. Pulling his last load from the dryer, he picked up his basket and headed down the hall to his apartment. As he came around the corner to his end of the hallway, he saw the figure of death sitting in the exact chair he had sat in the last time. Startled, the man dropped the laundry basket and backed up against the door of another apartment.

The hooded figure rose from his seat and gestured for him to move away from the door he was leaning on. Slowly, he stepped to the other side of the hall, and the door behind him opened. He felt a cold breeze drift from inside the room, and the ghosts of the couple who lived there stepped out and took death by the hand. Then they disappeared.

This second event frightened the man so much that he called his daughter in Florida. He shared his experience and was relieved to find that the girl was a very sympathetic listener. She never questioned or challenged his account of these terrifying encounters. Having the chance to talk through these experiences with her helped calm him down quite a bit. In fact, he went to bed and slept well that night.

In the morning, however, he was greeted by a knock at the door. In the back of his mind flashed a vision of death coming to his door. Reluctantly, he opened the door and was greeted by two women in smart-looking pantsuits and a young strapping lad in a white shirt and tie. All three of them had laminated ID badges. The large letters proudly posted along the top edge of these badges said "Evaluation Counselor," along with the local hospital logo.

The trio explained that his daughter had called with some concerns about how he was doing and that they just wanted to talk with him for a while. For the next hour and a half, he recounted for them his experiences but added that he hadn't been resting well and probably dreamed it all. The counselors left him with some reading material, a hotline phone number magnet for his refrigerator and a prescription for some sleeping pills.

From that moment on, he decided he would not relate these stories to another living soul. If it ever came up, he would insist that he dreamed the whole thing. As far as he or anyone else would ever be concerned, it never happened in the first place.

All was quiet after that. Perhaps he had only dreamed it. Things got better for him after that. He made new friends and grew comfortable with his new life in the retirement community. In fact, he got to the point where he would chuckle about the whole thing whenever he thought about it. The entire affair became a distant memory until one fateful night in October, a Halloween night, to be exact.

Every holiday brought with it some form of party or special dinner at the community room. It was Halloween, and there was to be a costume contest, sugar-free candy and special entertainment followed by a classic old scary movie. It was a big deal. The lobby was decorated high and low with ghosts, monsters, spider webs, zombie hands that offered jellybeans and a dozen black roses adorning the piano. Everyone was primed and ready for a good time.

Sadly, one of the man's new friends had fallen ill and could not come to the party. As the room began to fill up with vampires, witches, hobos, showgirls with feather boas and mummies, the man remembered his missing friend and gathered up some snacks to take up to his room in hopes that it would make him feel better.

As he passed by people to get the food, he received many compliments on his costume. He thought this was odd as all he had done was put on his old bowling team shirt from many years ago along with a ball cap from the bowling alley his team used to play in. He made his way out of the crowded party area and went up to his friend's room. He knocked, and his friend called out for him to enter. He opened the door, but before stepping in, he glanced into the reflection of an outside window. It was dark outside, so the windows became a kind of transparent mirror on the inside.

Looking up, he was startled to see standing right behind him and now entering the apartment the hooded figure of death that had not plagued him for months. Suddenly, he realized the compliments on his costume were for the shrouded specter that was standing beside him the entire evening. In the window, he saw death slip past him and close the door. He tried to open it again, but it was locked.

He went back to his apartment and refused to look back down that hall again. He vowed never to tell anyone of what he had seen. He took one of the sleeping pills and went to bed. The visions of death, his friend, the ghosts and that wing chair all melted together in his mind as he drifted off to sleep.

The next day, there was a card sitting out in the dining room. It was a sympathy card for the family of his friend. He felt guilty that he had somehow played a part in this by opening the door. But logic suggests that a locked door won't stop death from making his appointed rounds.

It was with a great deal of personal angst and a promise of anonymity that this story was related to me. Perhaps he dreamed it all. Or perhaps I met a man who has seen death sitting in a wing chair.

CHAPTER 9
THE FIELD LIGHTS

Here is a story that was reported to us in a variety of forms by a very diverse sampling of people. Old and young, natives and out-of-town ghost enthusiasts all offer up a version of this fascinating tale. But only one person was able to bring the strange manifestations in this ghost story together to a logical solution that is quite chilling.

There is an old field just outside the west side of town that is nothing but weeds and random bushes, bits of busted cement, a tipped-over tree and, off to one side, a homemade baseball diamond in a patch of dirt. The baseball diamond has been one of the main reasons so many people have had personal encounters with this ghostly apparition.

It seems that when the area of the field by the tipped over tree and the busted bits of cement is covered by fog, a mist of rain or smoke from nearby burning leaves or a neighborhood grill, one, two or three lights become visible over the area. In a heavy fog, they are especially visible and most disturbing.

These lights emanate from a single "hot spot" point and a literal beam of light, spreading ever-wider trails from this hot spot off into the distance. These lights are reported to be of varying heights from about three feet above the ground to ten feet above the ground, and the third light, when it is seen, is about fifteen feet off the ground.

The lights are always described as two of them facing north and the middle one facing to the south, exactly back at the other two. The beams of these lights are moving around, back and forth and up and down. It is a most extraordinary and shocking sight to behold.

I was told that there are videos of this phenomenon taking place on the Internet, but I found none that clearly showed the occurrence. Likewise, there are dozens of still photos, but it is very difficult to discern the details of these grainy, blurry photos.

There have been numerous theories as to how and why the field lights occur. One popular theory is that the lights are car headlights from the intersection back at the highway, several hundred yards away. The major problem with this premise is that it would seem that the origin point of the lights would clearly come from the intersection, not a fixed point over the lot, and it also fails to explain the middle light shining in the opposite direction.

Another concept designed to rationalize the event is that old broken glass or shiny stones on the ground among the cement and twigs and grass are reflecting starlight or ambient light from the city. The problem here is that the beams would clearly be coming up from the ground not hovering around and about the middle of the air.

A pseudo-scientific cause was written up in a local publication at one point. This explanation contends that certain properties of luminous or phosphorus gas or micro-particles are present in the atmosphere above the lot. The theory suggests that these elements have escaped up from the ground or wafted in from other unidentified sources within the adjacent neighborhood. When the moisture content or temperature shift above the surface is just right, then the particles appear to illuminate in midair.

The variety and scope of skeptical explanations demonstrate just how vexing the field lights are to those who have witnessed them. Due to these types of speculations, the field lights are considered an unsolvable atmospheric anomaly. However, the only explanation your present team of authors has encountered that makes sense of all these puzzling factors is a ghostly one.

A retired firefighter offered this recollection:

> *About ten years ago, there was a big, sprawling house on that lot. The house belonged to a real estate man who happened to own most of the cheap apartment complexes in town. It was a very ornate and fancy place, with landscaped walkways and a big tree just off the side of the garage. These folks lived there for years until the house was struck by lightning and set on fire. It was a bitter cold night in January. They had no close neighbors on that lot, so the fire had progressed pretty far by the time they noticed and called the fire department. When we arrived, the house was about halfway gone in the blaze. The family was standing outside holding*

flashlights, crying and huddling together. We had just gotten the hoses on the flames when a little boy broke free from the family and ran into the house screaming about something that was left inside. The dad and an older son ran past the firemen and into the house as well. Some firemen went in after them, but half the house collapsed the very same moment and the firemen retreated back out of the house. The chief used his bullhorn to order them out of the house, and for a moment you could see all three of them shining flashlights all around inside the house. The roof caved in on the other half of the house, and a huge plume of flames shot into the air. Right after that, the south wall fell in on top of the roof. By morning, all that was left of the house was a smoldering pile of debris. The police found that the father and his two loyal sons had been killed under the rubble. Two of them still had those flashlights in their hands, still on. So when I heard about the lights over the field, I realized that was the old foundation of the house and those three who died trying to find and save one another must still be searching for a way out. They never knew what hit them. Their ghosts are still determined to save each other. When the fog looks like smoke, you can see those lights searching and searching. I believe they are always there and have been there since that house crashed in on them. It's just that we don't see them without the fog. That is a haunted house once removed.

I have never heard any better explanation for the Springfield field lights. We hope these trapped, restless souls find one another at last, and may they rest in peace.

CHAPTER 10

THE ICY FINGERS OF DEATH

On the outskirts of the old north side of Springfield there are a lot of metal buildings. "Pole barns," as they are known in the real estate trade, are famous for being inexpensive and useful for a multitude of inelegant uses. Today, you will see many such metal-sided buildings that are being used as storage warehouses, skating rinks and car repair shops, among other things.

One of these locations formerly served as an icehouse near the railroad yards. The metal walls allowed for trucks to back in and out for pickup or delivery of ice chunks and slabs. The incoming ice slid down a huge chute to a storehouse below ground, where the ice could be kept at a low temperature. This highly insulated, dark area was the freezing cold heart of the icehouse business.

Springfield Ice House was an important aspect of the town's business development. It became an economic powerhouse, pivotal to not only local business but also to every operation that needed to ship produce, meat or other reactive goods out of Springfield to other cities by rail.

One of the workers, a so-called block buster by trade, was apparently the last man working one night. He carefully followed his closing time ritual to the last detail. He locked up the icehouse, put away all his tools and hung up his heavy overcoat and insulated waders. Somehow, he ended up in the wrong place on the upper level, became disoriented and stepped onto the ice chute. Immediately, he fell down the chute and through the wooden flap door and dropped fifteen feet onto some jagged shards of ice slabs that had been dropped down there many hours earlier.

Being thrust into complete darkness and incurring multiple severe injuries from his drop onto the ice and floor, we can only imagine how badly this man began to panic and how many failed attempts he made in an effort to get out of the ice pit. We will never know the desperate acts that may have been performed that night.

What we do know is that it was a full three days later when the weekend washout of the ice pit revealed the man's mortal remains on the bottom of the pit floor. They were remarkably well preserved. The ensuing investigation ruled that the man's demise was a workplace accident or, at the very best, "death by misadventure."

Ultimately, the icehouse closed, and other business operations stood over this subarctic burial plot. About 1970, the first whispers of a ghost story surfaced. At this time, the old icehouse was the warehouse for a carpet outlet store. Inside the building were wooden sections and divided levels, where huge carpet rolls could be lifted and stacked by forklift until they were called for by the sales manager. A dozen people worked in the warehouse, which was known for one outstanding feature, especially in the summer: it was murderously hot inside that metal pole barn.

The sheet metal walls had the effect of trapping the sun's warmth and amplifying it many times over. The long-suffering souls who worked inside the warehouse were frequently subject to dehydration, heat stroke and fainting spells. The heat, coupled with the hard physical nature of the labor going on in the warehouse, made it seem even funnier when one worker thought another worker standing in a doorway said, "Can you turn up the heat?" This phrase and others just like it became the office joke, and soon you could hear them just about all the time around the building.

It was during a lunch break when three of the employees were sitting on rolls of carpet drinking cold soda pop to cool off. Suddenly, all three of them heard quite clearly a voice directly in front of them say, "Please turn up the heat. It's so cold. Help me." This phenomenon repeated itself three times before the workers were completely unnerved and left the room in terror.

The bosses quickly dismissed this fantastic tale as being caused by the heat or a mischievous staff member trying to get time out of the sweltering shelter. Soon after that, the voice would be heard again on occasion, and other even more troubling things began to occur. A slow-moving fog or mist could be seen in the corner of the warehouse, and those who witnessed this oddity also reported that the entire room felt much cooler almost immediately.

Was this a ghostly manifestation of the man who died in torment while freezing to death beneath the floor? It is unclear if anyone associated with these stories from the early 1970s was even aware of the old icehouse and its fatal mishap. But it would seem that the iceman had indeed cometh—back from the dead in spirit form! He had been heard in the mysterious voice asking for warmth, and he had been seen in the form of the cold fog hovering near the ground. Is it any surprise that next he would be felt?

Years passed, and the carpet store eventually closed. The warehouse was emptied out and abandoned. It was then that an official report tied this place to the story of the ghost. On September 1, 1977, the Springfield police were summoned to the abandoned warehouse. Realtors were reposting a sale or lease sign late in the evening when they said they heard an angry voice hurling profanities at them from inside the structure. They immediately called the police.

When the police arrived, they banged on the outside of the building and shouted for anyone inside to leave. They called out that this was private property and anyone caught trespassing would be prosecuted. The big metal garage door handle clanged open and then began to rise. The police expected to see a homeless man or a juvenile delinquent of some sort apologize and walk sheepishly out. Instead, they saw no one standing behind the big iron door, but they felt a wave of very cold air waft out of the building and blow against them.

There are different versions of what happened next, but the overall account seems to suggest that they saw breathing in the middle of the doorway, breathing that was clearly visible in the air, like when a person is outside during the winter. This visible breath coincided with a panting sound. Supposedly, one officer stepped away from the others and walked in closer to these mysterious puffs of air. The officer looked left and looked right to see if he could spot a person hiding inside the warehouse. As the officer took a slow, deliberate step into the building, there was a loud scream, a burst of this visible breath and the officer was pushed to the ground, knocking the hat off his head. As the officer's body slid clear of the doorway, the big metal door slammed down and locked itself.

The police could reach no rational conclusion for what had happened. Ultimately, the report states that police entered the warehouse and a person ran from inside, shoving past an officer. The report says the intruder could not be identified. What other encounters that people may have had with this alleged ghost is unclear. After the 1979 incident, I have been unable to find any threads to later stories that could trace back to the original. Perhaps our ghost gave up after so many decades of frustration with the living. Or perhaps he lies in wait for the next person who dares to make his tomb into a business. Perhaps he has stored up all manner of horror for the next warm body that intrudes. Now that's cold.

CHAPTER 11
THE DREARY SIDE OF DRURY

In addition to the deeper story behind the mysterious music that pours from Clara Thompson Hall at Drury University, we find an old adage holding true: misery loves company, and one has to presume that ghosts are miserable souls. It is no surprise at all then to learn that Drury University has a few other skeletons rattling in its academic closets.

With so many reports of unholy activity on the premises, it gives one pause to wonder if there might be a greater force at work. What if there is a kind of "paranormal magnet" that keeps pulling supernatural events toward the university? Those who find clusters of alleged ghosts, countless reports of strange phenomenon spread out over a long period of time and coming from sources that are removed from one another by generations often discover a root cause of the haunting.

There are four ghost stories that have survived the test of time and diversity of witnesses at Drury University. Of course, there are countless other stories, some of which are not originated in ghosts or haunting but just silly pranks and college-level hijinks. However, these four locations have always been the subject of ghost stories. These are stories that have followed the same basic patterns, despite who is relating the experiences. I believe the last one may hold the key to understanding why the university continues to keep its old ghosts and, over time, collects new ones as well.

Wilhoit Theatre Lights

One of the most famously haunted places on campus is the Wilhoit Theatre. Inside this well-worn facility, students report strange noises coming from darkened areas in the building. Some have mentioned a menacing and oppressing presence or spirit that follows you through the auditorium. There are reports of certain people feeling cold, frightened or suddenly nauseous sitting in the audience, while the rest of the crowd is untouched. One young actress came out of the dressing room winching in pain and with deep scratches in the middle of her back.

But the most common manifestation of ghostly occupancy is a flicking on of lights throughout the entire building at night while no one is working or performing there. One may tend to be unimpressed at the idea of lights flickering in an old building as evidence of a haunting. Allow me to elaborate.

This is not a matter of a light flicking on and off again as it is seen through a window. When this occurs at the Wilhoit Theatre, an outside observer will see a light flicker and come on, somewhat like a fluorescent tube in a cold room. It flickers, flashes and then comes on steadily. But our outside observer would then see this happen in an area next to the original light, and after that light comes on at full strength, the first one will go out. In a matter of time, the light has moved from left to right and bottom to top and then out.

When I asked my ghost researcher associates what they thought of this, they told me it was a most unusual and rare kind of manifestation. If it is genuinely caused by ghosts, then it would be transformational energy surges that spirits give off as they make efforts in the material world. In other words, the energy of the spirit moving around the building is giving off enough electromagnetic energy to turn on the lights for a brief time. It would also mean you are seeing the path of the spirit when watching where the lights are turning on.

Some of the people who have been around the Wilhoit Theatre a long time have heard so many ghost stories that they have come to refer to the ghost as "Bob." Ironically, the theater is named after Bob Wilhoit. Do they know something we don't?

Smith Hall

In the mid-1960s, the university found itself with an ever-expanding student enrollment. To accommodate all the new attendees, it built Smith Hall on a part of the property that used to be a long series of residential Victorian houses. About a third of the way down this row of houses was an empty lot. The house that had stood there years before had burned to the ground.

Inside that house when it burned to the ground was a young girl holding on to a much-loved teddy bear. She failed to exit the house in time to avoid her tragic fate, as she was in search of this teddy bear. She found the bear but lost her life. The very place she died was the starting point for the construction of a women's dormitory.

Once Smith Hall was open for business, reports of strange incidents began pouring in, as well as complaints from girls saying they couldn't sleep because they felt nervous and anxious for no good reason when they were in their rooms at night. A rash of reports about some manner of peeping Tom made their way to the administration offices as well. Guards and sharp-eyed staff members were given charge to make sure no Toms would ever peep in Smith Hall. Despite the vigilance and the assurance that there was no one creeping about the dorm, the reports of feeling watched continued.

One day, a theft was reported inside the troubled building. No less than two young ladies hesitantly admitted that missing from their rooms were their teddy bears. That's when things started to get weird in Smith Hall.

Common tales related to the hall include returning to your room and finding your closet and drawers open or strewn across the room. Locked doors are frequently found standing open. Eventually, reports came to the office from girls who say they saw a little girl with a teddy bear wandering down the halls. In fact, at least one person on each floor made a similar report.

Sometimes a girl would wake up in the night and scream or gasp, swearing that she had seen this little girl standing by her bed staring at her. The little girl was always described as holding a teddy bear and wearing a pink satin dress.

A more frightening development emerged when a young lady was found dead in her dorm room. On her bed sat a teddy bear. Her friends all agreed it did not belong to her and that they had never seen it before. Can you imagine living in an environment where girls were afraid of the sight of a teddy bear?

This bear would occasionally turn up in another student's room. More often than not it would turn out to be a prank that someone would eventually admit to having set up. Sometimes, however, the bear seemed to have a mind of its own and turn up in impossible places, disappearing only to reappear again. To this very day, there are tales of the little girl and her bear.

THE SOCCER FIELD

We already told you the history and background of the Clara Thompson Hall and its phantom strains of music, so we will move on the fourth area of the university that has consistently had reports of paranormal activity. This one likely holds the key to the question of why the campus seems to hold on to its haunts and collect new ones over time.

The Drury University Soccer Field, located off Benton Street, has been a rich source of ghost stories since its completion. The most common tales involve ghostly figures traipsing back and forth across the field. These figures come in a wide variety of shapes and sizes, and they are described in various stages of dress. Sometimes they appear alone and other times in groups.

Those who use the field or attend events on the field complain regularly that a very uncomfortable presence comes upon them. The result is chills, discomfort, nervousness and nausea—the same symptoms that occurred in select audience members at the Wilhoit Theatre.

What explanation could there be? Well, the field was built over a Native American burial ground. Some of those ghostly figures on the field in various stages of dress are apparitions of the Indians who lived and died there. That's a charged situation, to put it mildly.

As if that weren't enough to heat up a supernatural stew, there is another fact equally volatile to the situation: the same ground was also a bloody battlefield in the Civil War. So let's throw some restless souls who died in our war on top of those who perished before. Can you even imagine what it must be like for these two groups to discover each other in that realm that is beyond the mortal coil?

Those who follow and chart the reports of ghostly, paranormal hot spots in our nation recognize the Drury University Soccer Field as a major lightning rod of activity. And so it would seem that the entire campus has the perfect history of suffering, bloodshed, passion, anger, fear and tragedy to fuel its ghosts and otherworldly guests for all time.

CHAPTER 12

The Bride under the Phelps Grove Park Bridge

Phelps Grove Park is a lovely place in Springfield. It is located in a darling little neighborhood with a very nice play and activity area for children and families, and there is a lovely little art museum. It's a perfectly lovely little slice of Springfield suburbia.

The residential housing that surrounds the park is very pleasant and a top-rated haven for couples and families. With all that love floating around the area, it's no surprise to learn that one of Springfield's oldest ghost stories is a tragic tale of lovers from days long gone.

Just how long ago, no one is willing to say. What were the names of the families involved? No one seems to know. Where are the physical remains of the players in this supernatural drama? No one knows that either. What we can say is that the theme and pattern of this story is to regional ghost stories as the works of Shakespeare are to classical literature: well established, predictable and over done.

You see, in terms of ghost stories, there are certain basic tales so universal that every city has its own version. The vanishing hitchhiker is a prime example. In this cookie-cutter format, a person driving along the road sees a hitchhiker and, by some sense of compulsion, picks him up. As they drive on, the hitchhiker reveals shocking information of some sort, most commonly that Jesus is coming soon or that the driver will die soon. After this information is conveyed, the messenger in the back seat just vanishes from within the moving vehicle.

Another classic ghost story is one that, as far as I can discover, goes back to a tale known as the "burning bride." In this story, you find a young mountain girl who is so excited about her wedding coming up the next day. Her mind is filled with thoughts of the wedding and the honeymoon. Lost in this fantasy of anticipation, she holds up her wedding dress in front of her and twirls around in the family's tiny cabin. On one of her twirls of elation, the dress swings over the open fire in the fireplace and catches alight. The wedding dress goes up in a dramatic blaze of flames, and the girl runs outside screaming in pain. She is never found, but the shimmering glow of her fiery ghost can still be seen sometimes at night.

In most places, the burning bride story is used by parents and grandparents as a cautionary tale. You see, the girl was foolish and was punished. She allowed herself to enjoy the idea of her upcoming happiness too much. This was an important belief in rural life, shaped by a very specific view of morality and sexuality, and so the burning bride is a cautionary tale to the culture.

Springfield's version involves a bride who is riding with her groom. She looked wonderful in her grand wedding dress and he in his suit, and they trot away in a horse-drawn carriage. The story goes that the groom became very jealous over his bride for some unknown reason. He was so jealous that he threw the horses into high gear, and as they crossed the Grove Park Bridge, the carriage overturned and flipped off the bridge. In the crash, the bride broke her neck. In a less common version of the story, she was completely decapitated.

Let's take a look under the hood of this little passion play. First, all we really can know from the few facts given is that passion, love and jealousy are dangerous, dangerous things. The occasion of a wedding symbolizes great joy and new pleasures. The accident means that sorrow will knock that giddy grin off your face in a hurry, so don't be so smug.

Another interesting fact is contained in the apparition that has apparently haunted Springfield in the aftermath of this tragedy. They say that on nights when the grounds around the bridge are misty or foggy, you can see the bride standing under the bridge. Her wedding dress is blowing in the wind, but in the place where her head should be, there is only darkness, with no visible support for her long, lovely veil.

If we look at the story as symbolic, the identity of the woman is erased. She has no face and no personal qualities at all. Is this a message to young girls that marriage will take your personal value and subjugate it to your husband and his actions and choices? Does that realization not temper your excitement over the wedding celebration?

Now, if on some misty, foggy night, curiosity finally gets the best of you, go ahead and wander out to the Phelps Grove neighborhood. Walk through the park until you come to the old cement-and-stone bridge. Take up your position at the top of the edge of the bridge, and look down toward the ground that goes beneath the bridge. If conditions are just right, and you are standing in just the right spot, you might catch a fleeting glimpse of the legendary bride under the bridge. If the spirits smile on you by giving you this experience, I want you to remember to not only gasp at the sight but also attempt to grasp at the meaning of it.

CHAPTER 13

THE INFAMOUS ALBINO FARM

The most sensational of all of Springfield's haunted places is the so-called albino farm. The first time I mentioned that I was collecting stories about Springfield for this book, I was met with wild-eyed enthusiasm with tales of the albino farm. I cannot count the number of folks who described with varying degrees of excitement all the terrible things that went on at the albino farm. It was the same as when friends tell you with great gusto about a horror movie they have just seen.

I was told about axe murders, suicides, torture rooms and human sacrifice. I was even told about a wartime experiment that resulted in a race of superhuman albinos. I discovered multiple books and Internet blogs about the infamous albino farm. I found wild cartoons and illustrations of a murderous, axe-wielding albino man in overalls.

I discovered a feature-length B-movie called *Albino Farm*. This indie film is very loosely based on the legend of this mysterious, now-abandoned property. The movie rolls out a parade of teenagers in peril, pig-faced rednecks with hay picks and nearly mutant-like albinos. At first, I thought it was a *Duck Dynasty* documentary, but alas, it is simply an over-sensationalized horror movie with all the aforementioned content. As of this writing, you can watch the entire cinematic delight on YouTube.

So just what is the history of this notorious place? Can we separate fact from fiction anymore? And even if you could, would it make any difference in the reports of ghosts and terrors that seem to flow steadily day after day?

I will attempt to present the known history of the family and the property. After that, we will look at the most established ghost stories and see if we can draw real threads from one to the other. Fasten your seatbelts; it's going to be a bumpy and bizarre ride!

You will find the albino farm if you travel out to Greenlawn Cemetery. Just north of the cemetery, you will find a road that turns off to the left. Journey down that road past a rock wall covered in overgrown vegetation. Shortly, you will come to what was the driveway. You will also notice that you cannot drive any farther, as the drive is barricaded by some sizeable rocks and boulders. The boulders are just one of the steps that have been taken to keep people off the grounds. These are the grounds of Springlawn Farms.

And here comes our first chance to analyze some information about this legendary location. Are the boulders there to keep you from discovering the horrors of the past and becoming the next victim of the demon souls who still roam the woods? Or are they there because many people have come out to the grounds looking for spooks and monsters and ended up being the victims of their own actions? You decide.

Long before rocks blocked the way to the house and plants had taken over the last remains of the walls on the estate, the original farm and house was built by none other than Springfield's postmaster and hotshot businessman, General C.B. Holland. The general built the house before the Civil War broke out.

Holland sold the property to a man named George McCaa`n. Strangely, the McCaan family was uncomfortable with the house and resold it after owning it only a very short time. Just what kept the family unsettled remains a complete mystery. Mr. Frank E. Headley Sr. bought it from McCaan in 1904.

The Headley family was known for operating a high-profile wholesale grocery business. Mr. Headley became the first person to start raising animals for market on the grounds of the farm. Only two years after buying the farm, Frank Sr. died unexpectedly, and the farm went to Frank Jr.

The younger Headley became very successful with his animal farm. He updated and modernized and expanded all the housing and animal husbandry facilities. He built a cement icehouse and huge mansion for his family to live in. He even added a park and a clubhouse, which was made from the logs used in the original cabin built by C.B. Holland.

In 1905, the property changed hands again to Mr. Mike Sheedy, who bought the existing grounds and several other adjoining properties. These acquisitions extended the property lines to over 1,200 acres. In 1923, the Sheedy family, numbering a total of nine people, moved in.

Mr. Sheedy became known for raising purebred short-horned cattle, as well as hogs and a great wheat crop. When he passed away, his family remained and kept up the business. When at last the final son died at a young age, the farm was left to the three Sheedy daughters. The girls were seen as somewhat helpless spinsters. They went through many sets of hired workers to keep the farm running, but alas, the family money was running out, and after some bad experiences with the workers, the farm failed.

The grounds of Springlawn Farm became overgrown and fell into a terrible state of neglect. In 1979, Helen Sheedy, the last of the Sheedy sisters, passed away and left the property and its "holdings" to her extended family members. Helen's family did not want anything to do with the farm. Either they had no interest in the huge task of restoring a massive farm operation, or perhaps there were other reasons they did not want the property. Within one month's time, everything that was associated with Springlawn Farm was up for auction. Everything must go!

In September 1980, a year after Helen's death, the house still standing on the property was burned to the ground. It was a spectacular fire that made news throughout Missouri. The only pieces left were the stone fireplace, the entryway stairs and the outside columns that flanked the big front doors of the house. It was a chilling and strange sight to see the columns and the stairway to nowhere leading up and over the fireplace hearth sitting on that burned, vacant foundation.

The cause of the fire was officially listed as arson. A suspect was pursued, but in the end, no arrests were made and no charges brought. Some see here a conspiracy to cover up the actions of a person who knew the horrible secrets the farm concealed over the years.

For all practical intents and purposes, that is the history of Springlawn Farm in Springfield, Missouri. So how do we go from Springlawn Farm to albino farms? This is where most of the folklore begins to take shape. Of course, there are traces of stories about why the second owner and his family didn't settle there. Was it set on haunted ground? Were there strange and frightening things already going on within the grounds? We are left only with conjecture.

We can know for certain that one of the bad decisions the three Sheedy spinster sisters made was hiring an albino caretaker to oversee the grounds and rest of the hired hands. This gentlemen was not only very disturbing to look at but also reportedly possessed a very bad temper. He was known for carrying his shotgun around the perimeter of the farm, firing at any and all trespassers.

An unconfirmed story says the man brutally mutilated two people walking over a local bridge. The story says he came up behind them and buried an axe in the back of one of them. He then beat the other with his bare hands and made the second person watch him chop up the first person. He then repeated the procedure on the witness. The suspicion is that he buried the bodies somewhere on the expansive grounds or fed the bodies to the cattle and hogs in their feed.

Another aspect of the legend states that the albino farm had a secret hospital that was hidden underground. Some suggest that the hospital was used during the Civil War days to treat Union sympathizers without notice. An alternate version of the story is that it was only allegedly a hospital to treat Union soldiers but was, in fact, a prison where soldiers were tortured and killed in sadistic ways.

The contemporary story is that a mad doctor had come back to this underground hospital and was performing wild experiments on several albino people. They say the result of the experiments is that the albinos went insane. This herd of crazed albinos went on rampages in neighboring farms and towns. They raped and murdered innocent citizens and kidnapped children who were taken back to the secret laboratory.

Some versions of the tale suggest that the albinos turned to cannibalism on these kidnapped children. They were also known to attack innocent passersby. The fear over walking past or on any part of the farm property grew among locals who were being treated to gloriously detailed accounts of these terrible deeds.

There are many other stories about Mr. Sheedy and his family. One of the best known suggests that Mike Sheedy hanged and killed himself in the dining room of the house. After that, one chair at the dining room table would fly across the room as the rest of the family tried to sit and eat together. Equally unsettling is the account of how his ghost roams the woods. If you should be unlucky enough to encounter his ghost in the woods, he will enter your mind and cause you to hang yourself as well. Another tale suggests that many hired hands throughout the history of the farm walked to a specific place near the icehouse and committed suicide.

Since the fire in 1980 drew fresh attention to the history and the folklore of the albino farm, paranormal activity rose dramatically. Reports of ghostly encounters, strange lights, noises, smells and even physical attacks on the grounds of the abandoned farm began to pour in. Soon after that, two groups of people began taking the haunted farm very seriously.

First, sincere investigators of the paranormal and supernatural, so-called ghost hunters, started visiting the grounds taking notes, electronic readings and hundreds of photographs and videos. All of this hoped to provide a basis of working information for any person or group interested in establishing what or who might be haunting the albino farm.

The second group was less focused in its goals. Local teenagers traipsed across the farm in the wee hours of the night looking for thrills. Oftentimes, the thrill seekers took their nervous dates out to look for spooks and monsters behind every bush and tree. It seemed to be a place to go to prove you weren't afraid. Of course, it also became a place for late-night teenagers to do what late-night teenagers are always looking for a place to do.

One documented case of strange noises and activity turned out to be three teens dressed in black who were simply lying in wait to scare the living daylights out of anyone who came out to see the farm. This proves how many people were visiting the farm at any given moment. Can you imagine the overgrown old farm with its swaying trees and cracking twigs under a moonlit sky and unbeknownst to a group of three or four people, they are passing within a hundred years of another group of three or four people who think they see, hear or feel "something out there"?

There was suspicion that certain groups of people were using the grounds for pagan rituals and witchcraft. This could well have been true, but there are no documents proving that authorities ever had dealings with such folks over usage of the farmland.

Many a ghost hunter has returned from a romp at Springlawn Farms with high readings on his or her EMF (electromagnetic field) meters and strange sounds on handheld digital recorders. To some, this is proof that all the stories are true, while others, perhaps a bit cleverer, say that even if none of the origin stories are true, the grounds are still haunted.

So let us bring this chapter to a close by admitting that sometimes places become so sensationalized that the absolute truth is hard—if not impossible—to find. Sometimes a place that is naturally old and scary isn't necessarily haunted. Until the ghosts start carrying identification and telling their whole histories, one cannot be exactly sure just what that creaking sound or the rustle in the bushes is.

Now, should you feel the deep need to go out to the grounds yourself, keep in mind that it is both dangerous and protected from trespassers. If you should run into a man with a very high-quality flashlight and a security badge, you may be arrested for trespassing. If, however, you are accosted by a tall, crazed albino man wielding an axe, you should probably just scream and run—and tell your story to as many people as possible the next day. Tradition!

CHAPTER 14

THE BLUE, THE GRAY AND THE BLOOD RED

Just a few miles to the southwest of Springfield lies a national historical landmark. It is Wilson's Creek Battlefield. This beautiful, green landscape was the location of the second major battle of the Civil War and the first major battle fought west of the Mississippi River.

The Civil War is one of the most romanticized wars in America history, with its proud Rebels and determined, industrialized Northern soldiers squaring off over a lifestyle that would be soon be "gone with the wind." It was, however, some of the bloodiest, nastiest fighting in our nation's entire war-rich history. The proximity of your enemy and the savage combat boggles the contemporary mind.

War today is a billion-dollar industrial science business. It's why we remain the land of the free and the home of the grave. We have put our considerable expertise to creating much more civil war. We have guns that can kill from amazingly long distances. We have drones that can kill entire neighborhoods and operate like video games. Today, you may never see the "whites of the eyes" of the person you are destroying. But in the Civil War, it was a much different matter.

Not only were you close to the action, but you might also actually know the person whose belly you just ripped open with a lead ball. The expression "brother against brother" was used to describe the Civil War, and in the case of Wilson's Creek, it was literally true for at least one soldier. Young Joseph Shelby of the Missouri State Guard and his stepbrother Cary Gratz of the First Missouri Infantry fought on the "Bloody Hill," and Gratz was killed.

Wilson's Creek is also the place where the first Union general was killed in battle. Nathaniel Lyon became a casualty of the Southern victory on August 10, 1861. Almost immediately, the pile of rocks that were used to mark the grave of General Lyon became a tourist attraction.

Today, the battlefield is one of the most pristine, beautiful parks in the United States. You can bring the family and enjoy the place where fellow citizens slaughtered one another whilst waving flags. The Civil War was unique in that it was fought on our soil, and we were our own enemy. These are just a couple reasons why the Civil War left such a severe scar on our national psyche.

It also explains why our beloved Civil War battlefields are hot spots for ghost sightings and paranormal phenomenon. As far as the ghostly world beyond the pale, here is a place where young men struggled, suffered and died miserable deaths. It's no wonder they would be restless.

I am unaware of any Civil War site that does not have an abundant supply of ghost stories. Wilson's Creek most often seems to produce visions of soldiers moving across the field. These semitransparent visions are sometimes accompanied by the sounds of gunfire and artillery. Voices of the soldiers rise along with strange mists that come from the ground and float for hundreds of yards until they return into the earth.

The dictionary defines "haunt" in a few ways. The primary definition is, of course, a place where the spirit of a deceased person continues to dwell. But the secondary definition also mentions "an unpleasant and recurring memory." The Civil War will always haunt America.

CHAPTER 16

THE COLONEL'S SECRET RECIPE FOR TERROR

One of the showcase businesses for Springfield is the University Plaza Hotel and Convention Center. This magnificent structure is designed to greet visitors and make a grand first impression for the city. It is a state-of-the-art hotel with world-class food, great service and even an in-house spa.

But there is one more thing you get when you stay at the Plaza that is not on the brochure or the website. You may well catch a glimpse or have a visit from "the colonel." Who, you may ask, is this gregarious guest, and why is he so ever present? It would appear that the colonel is the University Plaza Hotel's very own ghost. His title comes from his trademark appearance in southern attire, much like a famous fried chicken icon.

The colonel has been known to appear in the hallways, turn a corner and vanish. He has been reported to the front desk as being inside people's rooms. He is described as dressed in black and very calm but with an intense quality about him. Hotel guests find him sitting in a chair in their room when they return from an evening out. Even more disturbing, he may be discovered when you awake in the morning, sitting in that chair. But don't worry—once you startle and grapple for your phone, he will simply disappear.

One of the more famous episodes involving the colonel occurred when a brand-new employee encountered the colonel several times in one night. He saw him in the dining room, he saw him on the fourth floor, he saw him sitting in the lobby and he saw him in the bar. When this newbie mentioned to his supervisor that "the guy in black sure gets around here," he was sternly told not to talk about that man, to leave him alone and to never, ever, under any circumstances talk to him.

It was only later that other employees let him in on the secret that the colonel was a ghost. Shocked and scared by his close encounters of the supernatural kind, he quit his job. I can't say that I blame him.

The local history seems to indicate that the hotel now stands on ground that was once a big Southern plantation that was burned during the Civil War years and the colonel was a peace-loving pacifist who refused to take sides and fight in the war. For this resistance, he was lynched and his family killed by Confederate sympathizers. And so this lost soul roams the hotel that has planted itself on top of his home.

There have never been any stories about the colonel doing anything harmful or malicious toward anyone. The hotel insists that there is no colonel and that the million-dollar palace is not haunted. The ghost could no doubt be seen as bad for business. In my mind, the hotel should embrace this long-standing guest and use him in its marketing, perhaps in a slogan that goes something like this: "the University Plaza Hotel and Convention Center, a modern experience where a part of the old South still lives on." Win-win.

CHAPTER 16

Making Contact with the Guests

Just off Highway 44 at North Glenstone Avenue sits the Bass Country Inn. This durable old favorite hotel has made people feel at home for years. In fact, it seems to be so good at making everyone feel a part of things that some won't leave: ever!

A former busboy name Carl is a well-documented ghost who, despite his having died of a rare illness while still a teenager, still shows up for work every day. Carl has been spotted by staff members who knew him when he worked there—or rather, when he was alive and worked there.

Carl has been seen tending to business through the kitchen area and down the halls. Carl was in training to be a secondary worker on the industrial dishwasher system. Sometimes the sprayer will come on and move back and forth just as it does when someone is using it. Soon after that shocking scene, Carl will be seen again passing quickly through the kitchen storage area.

Workers assigned to clean up the break room have said that if they bend over to pick up trash or an object that has fallen off the table, they will see Carl's legs fully visible under the table though no one is seated there. This apparition has been noted in the dining room as well, and servers are firmly instructed never to visibly react to the sight. They are to report it to their shift supervisor immediately but not to attempt to do anything about it.

Carl apparently has a girlfriend in the great realm that lies beyond. He is often spotted going down the hallways of the hotel with a young lady beside him. Now, Carl's ghost has never acted aggressively toward any staff or guests. The same cannot be said for his spirited companion. Her temperament is rather volatile, and she has been known to shove past people in a crowded doorway or elevator.

The management always stressed to the employees the importance of making a personal connection and contact with the guests. Now, much to their chagrin, Carl carries on this special level of customer service today. So next time you stay at the Bass Country Inn, keep the corner of one eye out for the young busboy who lives to serve you from beyond the grave.

CHAPTER 17
UNCIVIL WARRIORS

Standing with a sense of imposing Old World dignity is the Springfield National Cemetery. At the corner of East Seminole and Glenstone Avenues, behind an ornate gated wall, is this cemetery (mostly) dedicated to the fallen warriors of the Civil War. In the center of the impressive collection of headstones is a tall monument to the soldiers of our bloodiest domestic exercise in destruction.

This historic site is also a place reportedly teeming with ghosts. Visitors claim to have seen and photographed glowing orbs floating all across the grounds over the graves. Sometimes the tombstones glow a bright green color and the letters of the names a deep moonlight blue.

The most sensational ghost that has been repeatedly seen and heard is a long black mist that rises from the midst of the graves and takes on human shape. As this mist passes near a person, he or she will claim to have heard the voice of an older man with a very Southern accent. What he is saying has never been discerned or recorded, but the fact that he speaks as he passes has been consistently reported by many diverse witnesses.

As we pointed out in an earlier chapter, the Civil War is an almost limitless source of ghosts and ghostly tales in America. Such tragedy and passion makes a logical case for these souls to be tormented and restless. Among the most notable alumni of the Civil War buried in the Springfield National Cemetery is Orion P. Howe. Orion was a unique part of the Civil War. He joined the war effort when he was twelve years old. Let that sink in. A twelve-year-old boy was part of the army. One day, it seemed to his commander that Orion was little and—dare I say—expendable enough to send across a battlefield to retrieve some badly needed ammunition. Orion and a group of other men were sent to fetch a supply of .54-caliber cartridges. The ammo unit set about the task. The other men were killed along the way, but little Orion somehow made it through. He was only severely wounded. The best part is that he was asked to bring the wrong size of ammo. It was, in fact, .59-caliber cartridges that were needed, not the .54-caliber ones that were delivered at such a high cost. Oh, well. That's military intelligence. After a long recovery, Orion became the youngest recipient of the Medal of Honor. He was a decorated soldier at the age of twelve years old. He had a Medal of Honor and a "red badge of courage." At this point, you may think young Orion has become an older, wiser man with battle scars. However, he reenlisted for service again and participated in another fourteen battles.

For his remarkable deeds, the military command chain sent word of his unflinching dedication to President Abraham Lincoln. Lincoln made special arrangements for Orion to go the Naval Academy, but he was unable to graduate. Eventually, he was sent to dental school. He settled in Springfield and died at the age of eighty-one. Orion Howe is just one more example of the kind of experiences that might fuel the haunting of Civil War cemeteries, monuments and battlefields.

One of the funniest ghost stories I ever heard also originated in this cemetery. The story goes that a man from Washington, D.C.—allegedly a well-known political muckity-muck you would recognize on the nightly news—was vacationing in Branson. He and his entourage came down to Springfield to make a speech before a political action group. The after-party went on a long time, and this minor celebrity/world leader was drunk as a skunk.

As the limo was leaving town with the inebriated statesman and his assistants in tow, they passed the cemetery. When this man saw the Civil War monument standing high above the fence line, he demanded that the limo driver stop and let him out. Soon it became apparent that his intent was to go into the cemetery and relive himself on the monument of the Confederate soldier.

Those in the car were laughing and giggling as he made a bad landing on the other side of the fence and proceeded to stagger toward the monument. In a moment, you could hear the audible proof that he was carrying out his mission. Everyone laughed and laughed, but the mood changed when they heard the man's voice crying out in protest. They heard the unmistakable sounds of a scuffle going on behind the fence, followed by the view of this man flying up and over the fence and landing with an unceremonious thud on the ground.

The headlights clearly illuminated the space behind him through the fence rails, and there was no one visible in the cemetery. Was this reprehensible elected official tossed out of the cemetery by a self-respecting, patriotic ghost? The man seemed strangely sober after that—a problem he took care of as the limo resumed its route to the airport.

CHAPTER 18

THE DORM MOM FROM HELL

"A loud pounding on the door that startles everyone living on the entire floor!" That's the way students describe the frequent attack of a most unwelcome and judgmental female ghost that prowls the Freudenberger House dormitory on the campus of Southwest Missouri State University.

The building plays host to the Military Science Department, along with over seven hundred students. The structure opened in 1959 and was named in honor of Norman Freudenberger. Mr. Freudenberger had been a professor of Latin for forty-five years at the university.

Somewhere over the course of the next twenty years, a female ghost began making it her duty to police the dorm. She paid special attention to the fifth floor. It became apparent that this spectral dorm mom was a stern taskmaster and expected absolute moral behavior from the girls in residence.

The dorm mom would pound and interrupt young lovers. She would adjust your thermostat and, in recent years, has taken to slapping laptop computers shut when they are browsing questionable websites. Only a few people have ever claimed to see the dorm mom in action. Those who have provide fairly consistent descriptions. She is an older, heavy woman in a worn purple dress. She has on black, thick-soled shoes and eyeglasses that turn up at the corners. These are styles not altogether inconsistent with those of the late 1950s or early 1960s.

The most unusual thing about a manifesting ghost with these habits is that no one is aware of a back story that might fit her into the role she is playing. There are no records of accidental deaths of mothers or dorm workers who would fit her description. No famous suicides or tragedies. There is nothing in the past to give us an easy thread from a previous event to the current mission of this phantom disciplinarian. As of right now, the dorm mother from hell is the most enigmatic ghost we have included in this book.

CHAPTER 19

The Sweet Monsters Sleep in Springfield, But They Play in Branson

Branson, Missouri, bills itself as the "live entertainment capital of the world." Backing this brag is the fact that there are more theater seats in Branson than New York City. Most of those seats are empty, but they are there. A lot of those empty seats are bolted to the floors of theaters that are closing or reselling again and again. Branson's entertainment has been influenced by big-name celebrities who virtually raced one another to name bigger and bigger buildings after themselves in the 1990s. As those days began to fade, the town resorted to sporting mostly revue show fare, such as one might see at an amusement park.

The town also sports a grand image of fundamentalist Christianity, with giant-sized replicas of the Ten Commandments greeting you as you roll into town. The version of Christianity that greets you in Branson is the southern America version, in which Jesus loves guns and stares suspiciously at outsiders. I had a friend who lived in Branson for a year who described it as a "snow globe with no water in it." As for me, I have been a professional magician for over twenty years, but the most complex and deceptive illusion I have ever seen is the city of Branson.

There was a time when a true original had an inspired vision for this sleepy little town. Long before *Sixty Minutes* broadcast its now-legendary feature story on the Highway 76 music scene that led to an unparalleled explosion in tourism, there was a man, two women, a theater, some monsters and a ghost.

Springfield was the burgeoning town in Missouri in the early 1930s. But just a little over thirty miles north of Springfield in Taney County was the city of Branson. At this point, Branson was a tiny, very rural town full of lakes and crazy dirt roads that wound their way higher and higher into the elevation of the Ozark Mountains.

It was also the domain of a very clever marketing genius named James Owen. James owned a drugstore and a car dealership, he was president of a bank, he was an outdoor correspondent for the Little Rock–based *Arkansas Gazette*, he manufactured a signature line of dog food, he ran a dairy farm and he ultimately served as the mayor of Branson for twelve years.

But his claim to fame would be his greatest business creation: the Owens White River Float Trip. In a very short time, the enterprising Mr. Owen had kindled a fire of national attention under Branson. Soon, he had the biggest and most successful float trip boat business in the country. He is the principle player in the creation of the modern Branson vacation industry.

To complement the river rides, fishing exhibitions and camping, he built an amazing building just a couple blocks from the water's edge. On Commercial Street, his Hillbilly Theatre was a remarkable structure. It was built with stone walls to mimic a cabin in the woods. The interior walls had no windows but recessed areas that looked like windows were actually painted by an innovative female artist named Elsie Bates Freund. Elsie operated an art gallery on a portion of the same property and eventually gained fame for her creations of jewelry using stones and metals.

James Owen called Elsie his "Hill Girl." Together, they opened the Hillbilly Theatre in 1936. It was the first theater in Branson, and it brought movies and live entertainment to tourists and locals alike. It attracted thousands of people and became the cornerstone of all the entertainment that would spring up in later years.

Through the determined efforts of Mr. Owen, the recreational opportunities available in Branson caught the attention of movie stars, socialites and other celebrities. They relaxed on the river and always came to the theater for entertainment. Charlton Heston, Gene Autry and others became regular fixtures throughout the years. Among the folks hobnobbing around the Hillbilly Theatre on a regular basis was eccentric artist Rose O'Neill.

Rose O'Neill had become a very famous and wealthy woman for her illustrations of what she called her "sweet monsters." The monsters were a kind of bizarre yet appealing merge of the god Pan and the faun. Many of these illustrations were provocative in that these manlike beings were usually nude in a setting of normal folk looking on. It was a most unusual vision and one that was a remarkable artistic success.

That success was only exceeded by her most famous creation, the Kewpie. This adorable yet haunting naked little baby with a wry smile became a top-selling toy and collectable. There were Kewpie books and games, and just about anything that could have a Kewpie on it did. Based on an illustration she did in 1909, Kewpies became an empire for Rose.

She led a very unorthodox life. She was married and divorced multiple times, chose to remain childless and, even as her Kewpie fortune faded, she supported her entire family and helped other artists through the Great Depression. Her happiest days were spent at her grand estate called Bonniebrook, which is located between Springfield and Branson.

Rose became a regular patron of the Hillbilly Theatre and one of its most spirited guests. Rose would help James Owen and "Hill Girl" greet the audiences and had a way of making any gathering into a party. She would sing and joke with everyone and clown for the regulars. She had been seen gliding across the edge of the stage in front of the movie screen. Sometimes she would get in the wings of the stage and sing until someone recognized her voice. It's safe to say that Rose's lust for life was satisfied during many of her visits to the theater.

In 1941, Elsa Bates and her husband, H. Louis Freund, moved to Eureka Springs, Arkansas, where they bought the house that belonged to the axe-wielding famous prohibitionist Carry Nation and started the arts colony that shaped the future of that famous city.

James Owen continued to build and exploit his float trip business and improve the business of Branson until he died of a massive heart attack in 1972. Elsa Bates Freund died in 2001 and is buried in her beloved town of Eureka Springs. Rose O'Neill died in 1944 and is buried on the Bonniebrook estate grounds.

But this is a book about ghosts, and I'm glad to tell you that while the old Owen theater has undergone many "demotions" in terms of its importance and prestige in the city, the stone lady still stands. After years of fading away, the Owen is on its way back to prominence with a full "boatload" of sensational entertainment.

There is, however, one more connection to the glory days gone by. Local ghost researchers believe the ghost of Rose O'Neill continues to enjoy herself at the theater. Her voice and her presence seem to be concentrated in and around the ladies' restroom. It is fitting that the member of that original team who was the freest spirit might leave a residual imprint of that spirit on the place she loved so much. May Rose and her visions of sweet monsters and Kewpies bring joy and happiness to a new generation of visitors to Branson, Missouri.

About the Authors

This is the third book by Edward and Karen Underwood. Their previous works, *Forgotten Tales of Arkansas* and *Haunted Jonesboro*, are also available from The History Press. They are entertainers, writers and historians of the more bizarre side of life.

Edward is an award-winning magician and storyteller. He also plays bass. Karen is a singer-songwriter and plays over a dozen musical instruments. You can find the latest performance information about them at www.remarkablearts.com

This is the first book project by John and Sherry Jones—you know, if you're trying to keep up with the Joneses. John is an experienced property manager. Sherry is also an experienced property manager but loves dogs more than property. They have two dogs and have plans for more in the future. They both love all things haunted and historical.